Kill My Mother

Kill My Mother

A Graphic Novel

Jules Feiffer

Liveright Publishing Corporation

A Division of W. W. Norton & Company

New York   London

Copyright © 2014 by B. Mergendeiler Corp.

For information about permission to reproduce selections from this book,
write to Permissions, Liveright Publishing Corporation,
a division of W. W. Norton & Company, Inc.
500 Fifth Avenue, New York, NY 10110

For information about special discounts for bulk purchases, please contact
W. W. Norton Special Sales at specialsales@wwnorton.com or 800-233-4830

Manufacturing by Four Color Print Group
Production managers: Anna Oler and Joe Lops

Library of Congress Cataloging-in-Publication Data

Feiffer, Jules.
Kill My Mother : a graphic novel / Jules Feiffer. — First edition.
pages cm
ISBN 978-0-87140-314-8 (hardcover)
1. Noir fiction. 2. Graphic novels. I. Title.
PN6727.F4K55 2014
741.5'973—dc23
2014005844

Liveright Publishing Corporation
500 Fifth Avenue, New York, N.Y. 10110
www.wwnorton.com

W. W. Norton & Company Ltd.
Castle House, 75/76 Wells Street, London W1T 3QT

1 2 3 4 5 6 7 8 9 0

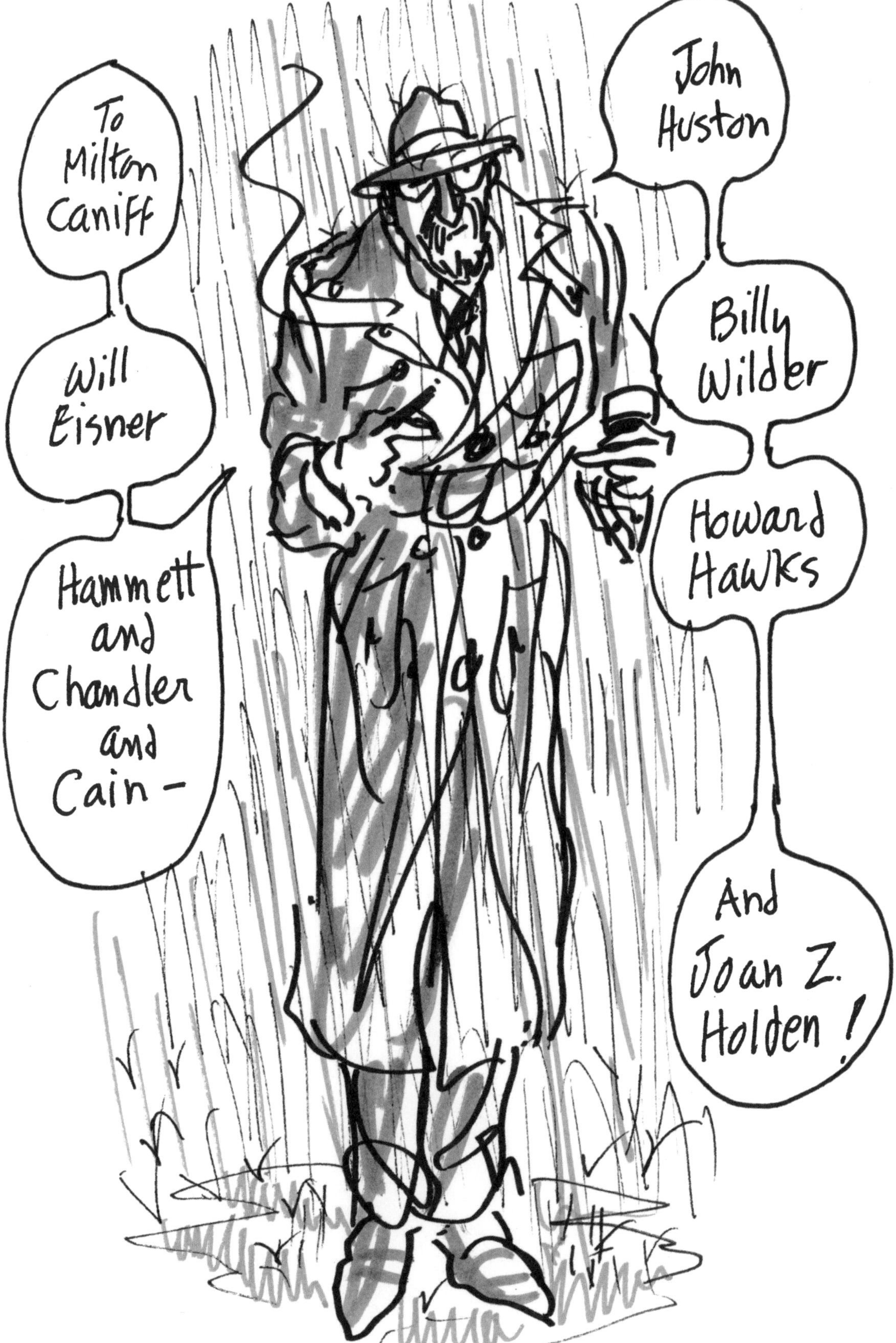
To Milton Caniff
Will Eisner
Hammett and Chandler and Cain -
John Huston
Billy Wilder
Howard Hawks
And Joan Z. Holden!

Kill My Mother

Part One:

Bay City Blues
1933

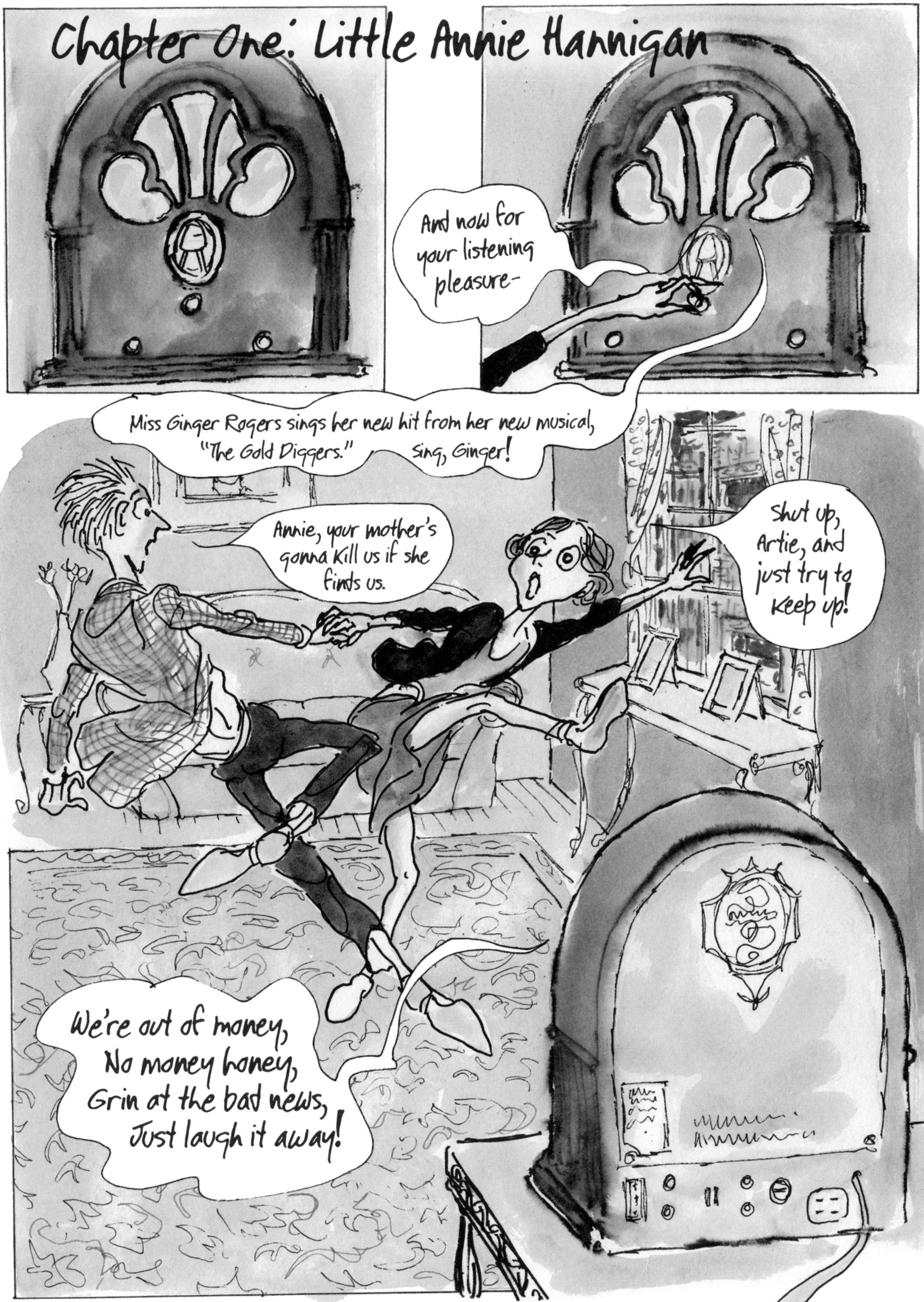
Chapter One: Little Annie Hannigan
And now for your listening pleasure-
Miss Ginger Rogers sings her new hit from her new musical, "The Gold Diggers." Sing, Ginger!
Annie, your mother's gonna kill us if she finds us.
Shut up, Artie, and just try to keep up!
We're out of money,
No money honey,
Grin at the bad news,
Just laugh it away!

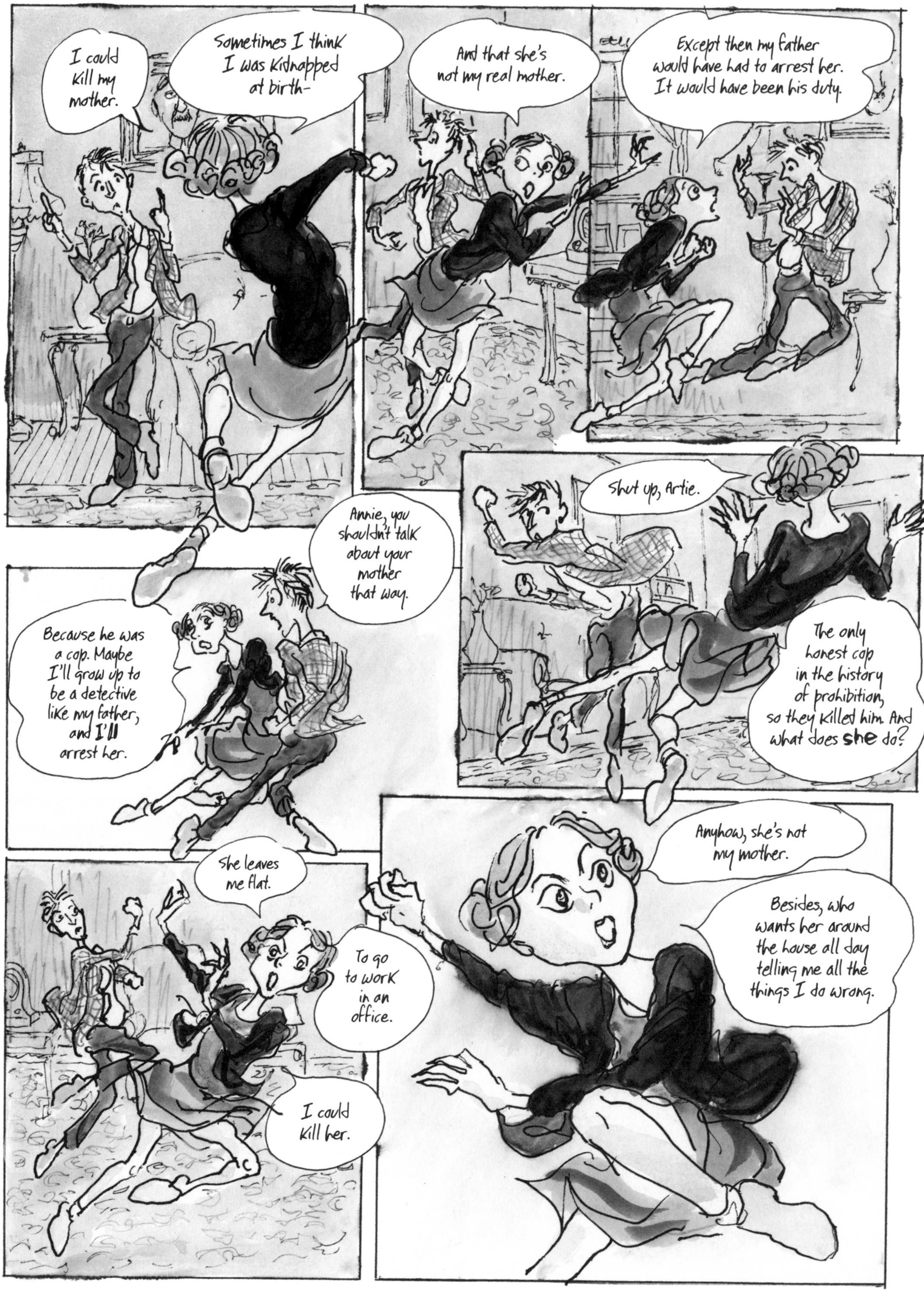
I could kill my mother.
Sometimes I think I was kidnapped at birth-
And that she's not my real mother.
Except then my father would have had to arrest her. It would have been his duty.
Annie, you shouldn't talk about your mother that way.
Because he was a cop. Maybe I'll grow up to be a detective like my father, and I'll arrest her.
Shut up, Artie.
The only honest cop in the history of prohibition, so they killed him. And what does she do?
She leaves me flat.
To go to work in an office.
I could kill her.
Anyhow, she's not my mother.
Besides, who wants her around the house all day telling me all the things I do wrong.

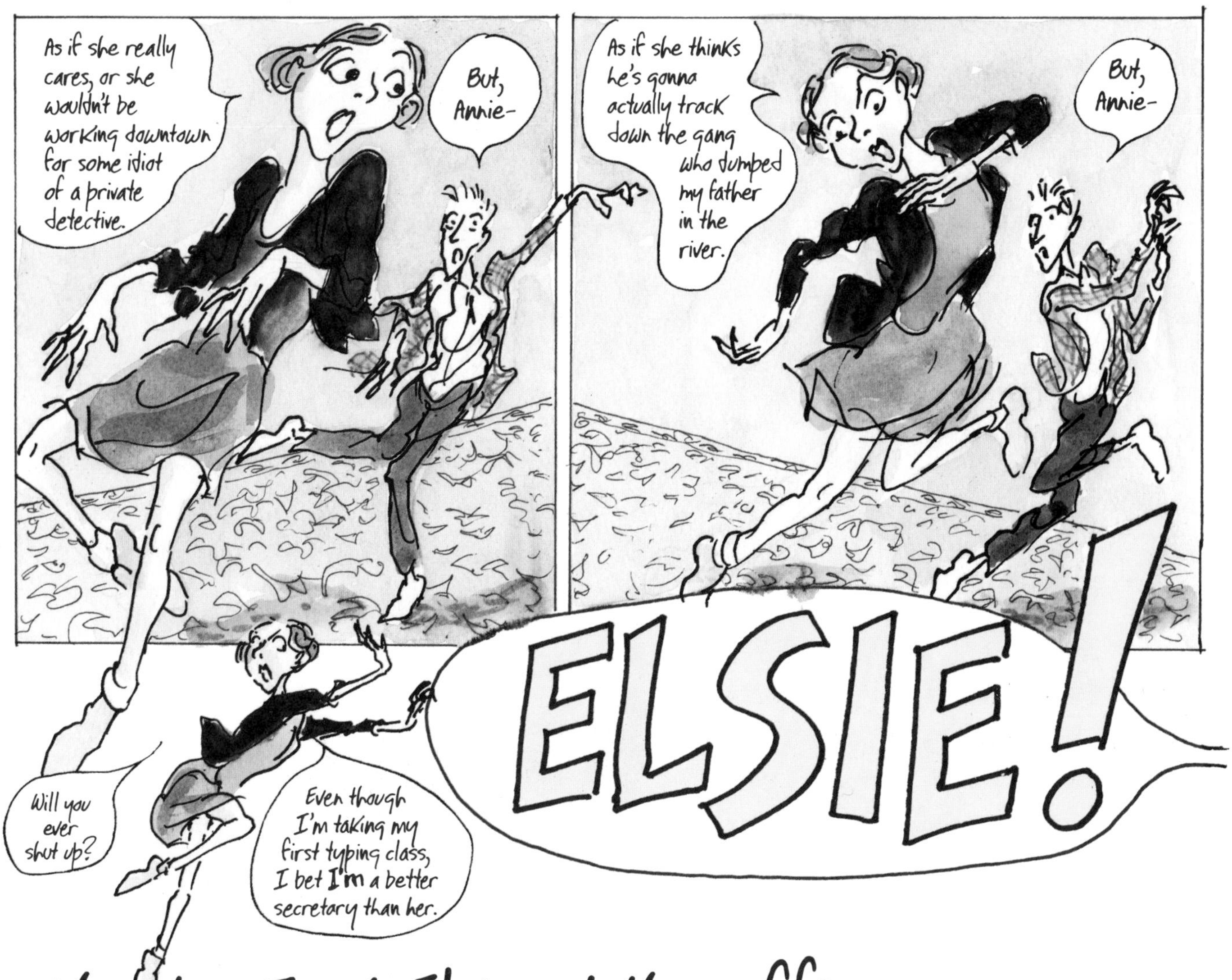
As if she really cares, or she wouldn't be working downtown for some idiot of a private detective.
But, Annie-
As if she thinks he's gonna actually track down the gang who dumped my father in the river.
But, Annie-
ELSIE!
Will you ever shut up?
Even though I'm taking my first typing class, I bet I'm a better secretary than her.

Chapter Two: Elsie at the Office

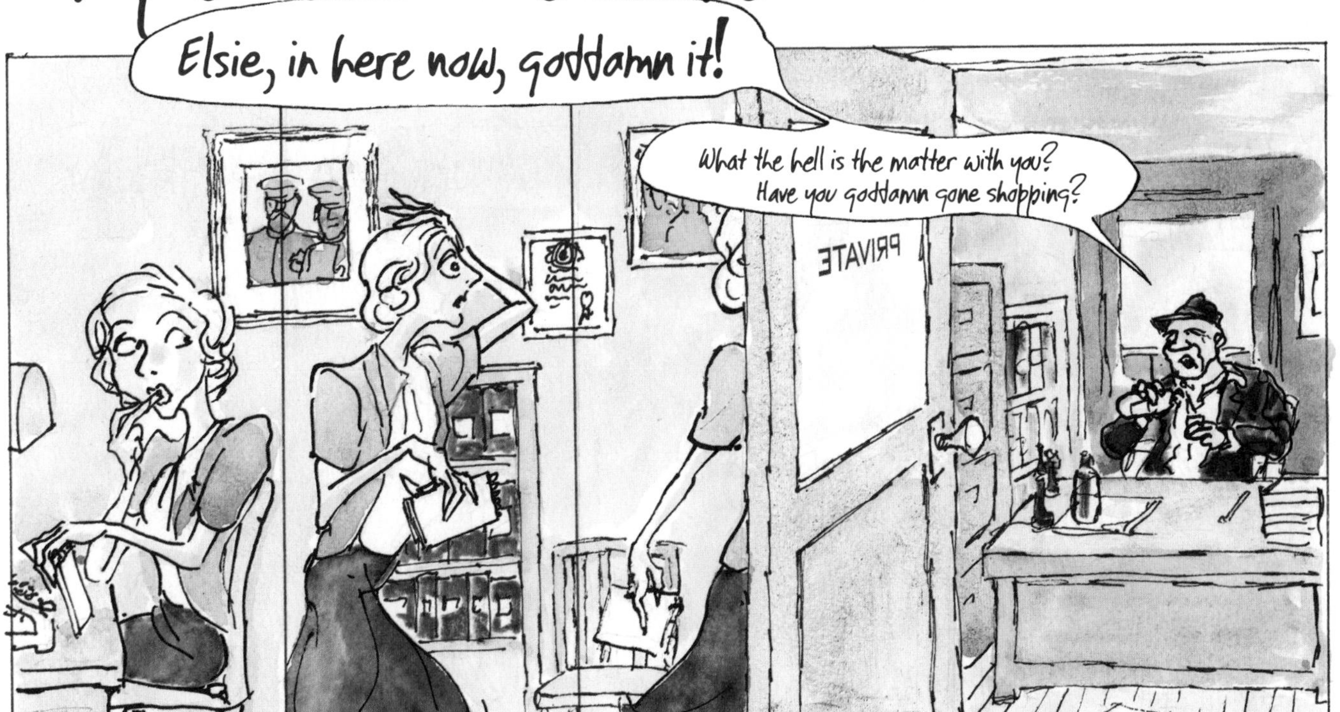
Elsie, in here now, goddamn it!
What the hell is the matter with you? Have you goddamn gone shopping?
PRIVATE

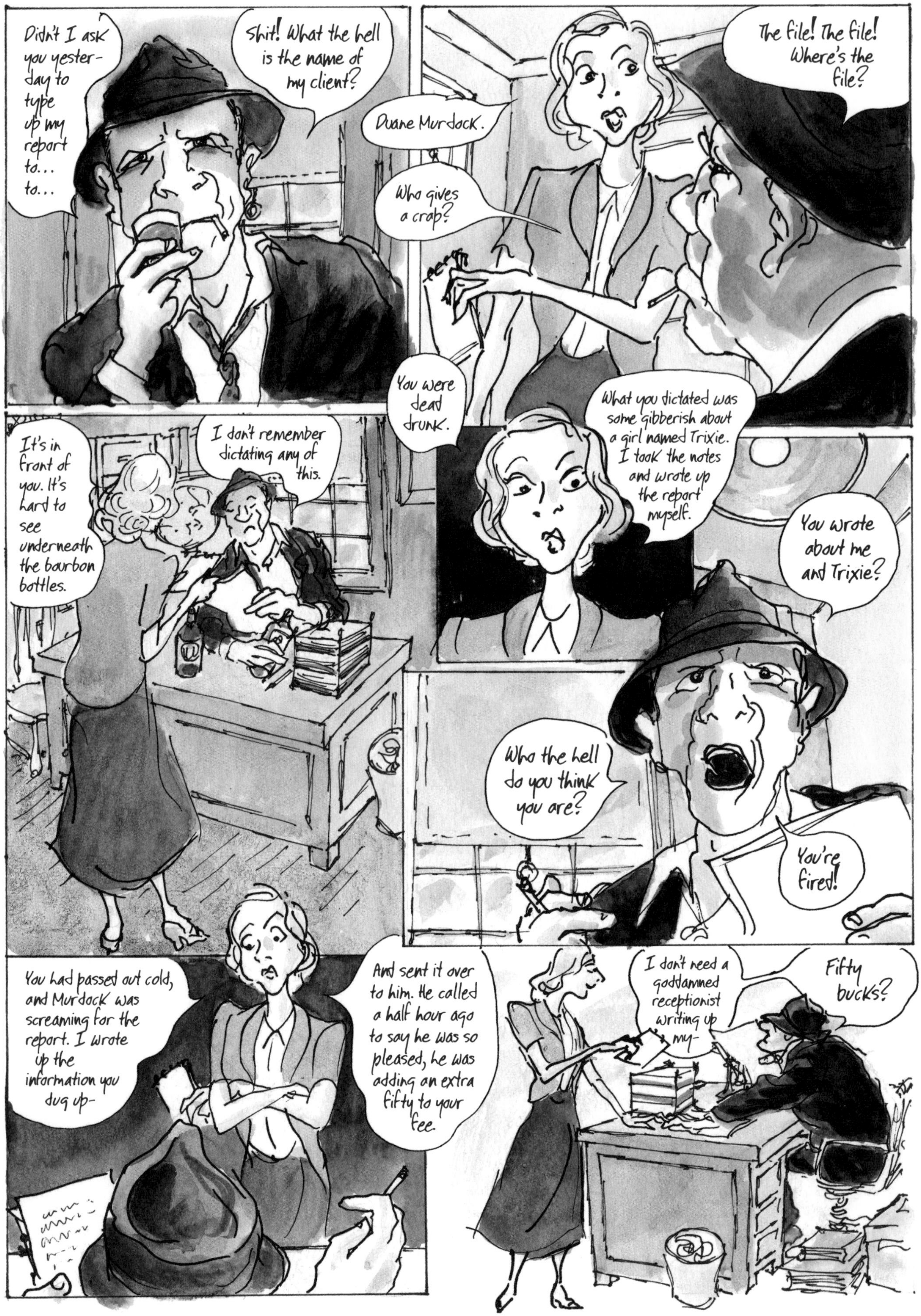
Didn't I ask you yester-day to type up my report to... to...
Shit! What the hell is the name of my client?
Duane Murdock.
Who gives a crap?
The file! The file! Where's the file?
You were dead drunk.
What you dictated was some gibberish about a girl named Trixie. I took the notes and wrote up the report myself.
It's in front of you. It's hard to see underneath the bourbon bottles.
I don't remember dictating any of this.
You wrote about me and Trixie?
Who the hell do you think you are?
You're fired!
You had passed out cold, and Murdock was screaming for the report. I wrote up the information you dug up-
And sent it over to him. He called a half hour ago to say he was so pleased, he was adding an extra fifty to your fee.
I don't need a goddamned receptionist writing up my-
Fifty bucks?

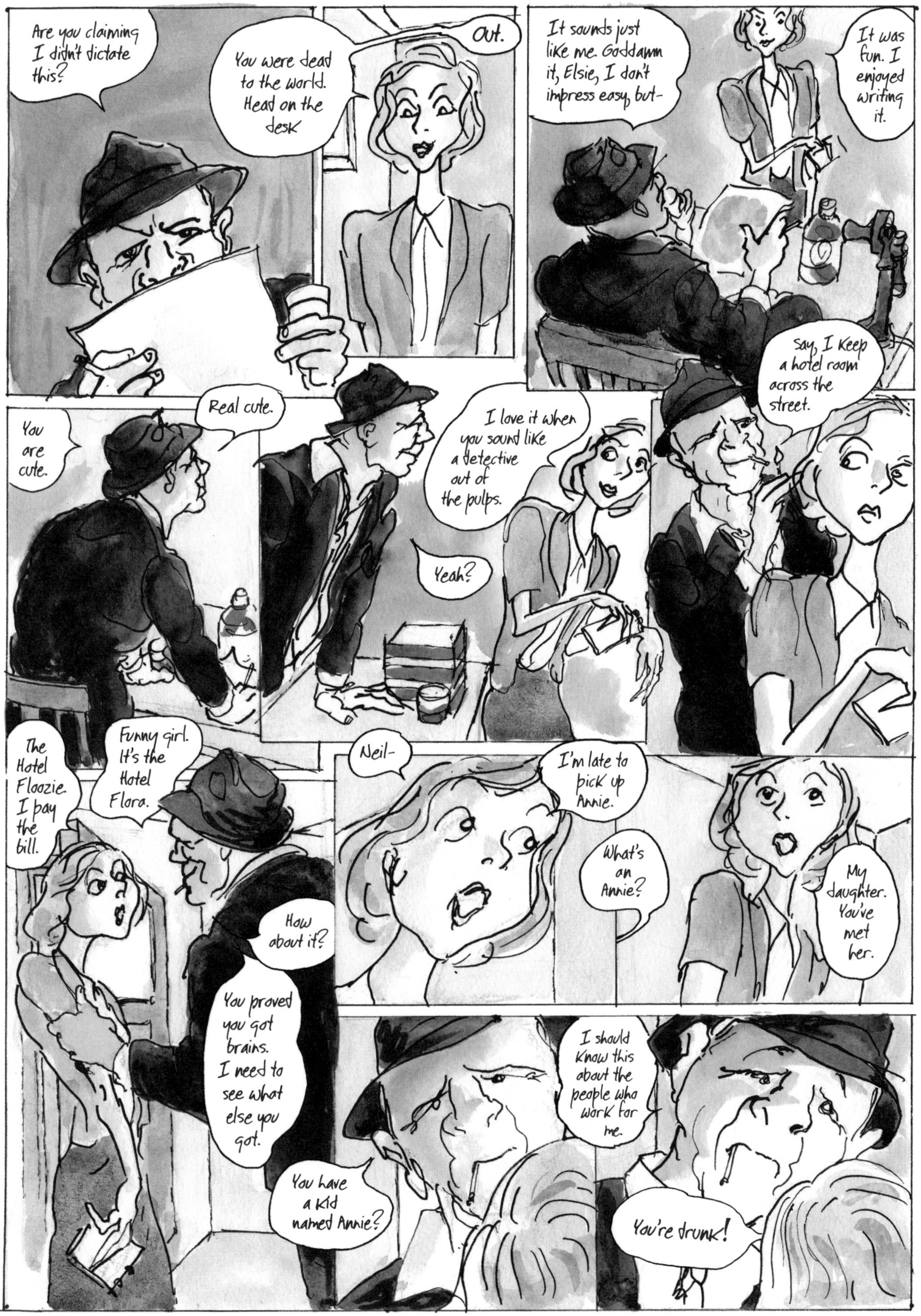
Are you claiming I didn't dictate this?
Out.
You were dead to the world. Head on the desk
It sounds just like me. Goddamn it, Elsie, I don't impress easy, but-
It was fun. I enjoyed writing it.
You are cute.
Real cute.
I love it when you sound like a detective out of the pulps.
Yeah?
Say, I keep a hotel room across the street.
The Hotel Floozie. I pay the bill.
Funny girl. It's the Hotel Flora.
How about it?
You proved you got brains. I need to see what else you got.
Neil-
I'm late to pick up Annie.
What's an Annie?
My daughter. You've met her.
You have a kid named Annie?
I should know this about the people who work for me.
You're drunk!

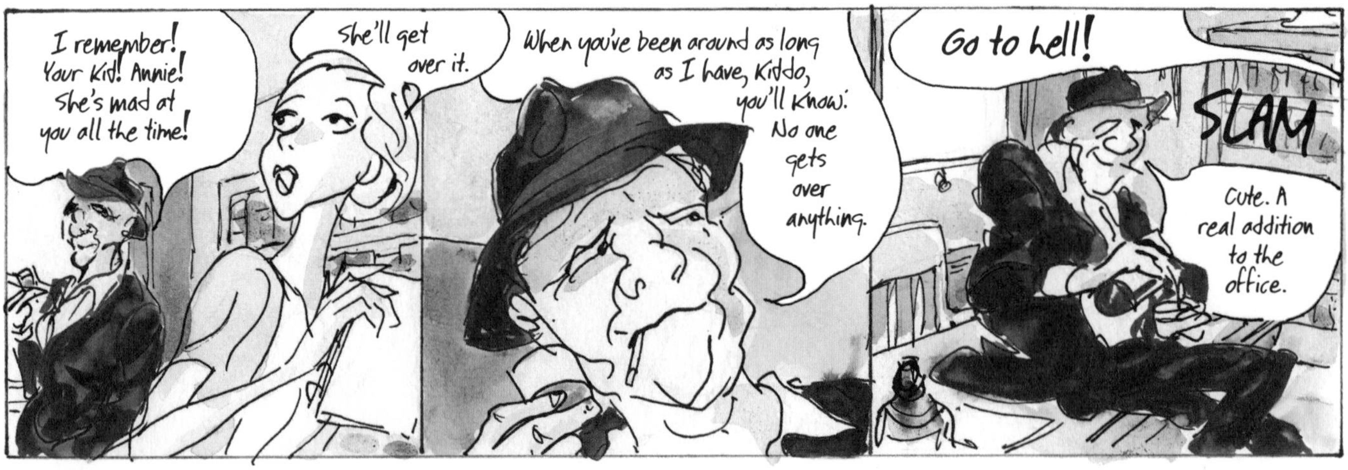
I remember! Your Kid! Annie! She's mad at you all the time!
She'll get over it.
When you've been around as long as I have, Kiddo, you'll Know: No one gets over anything.
Go to hell!
SLAM
Cute. A real addition to the office.

Chapter Three: The Tattoo Artist

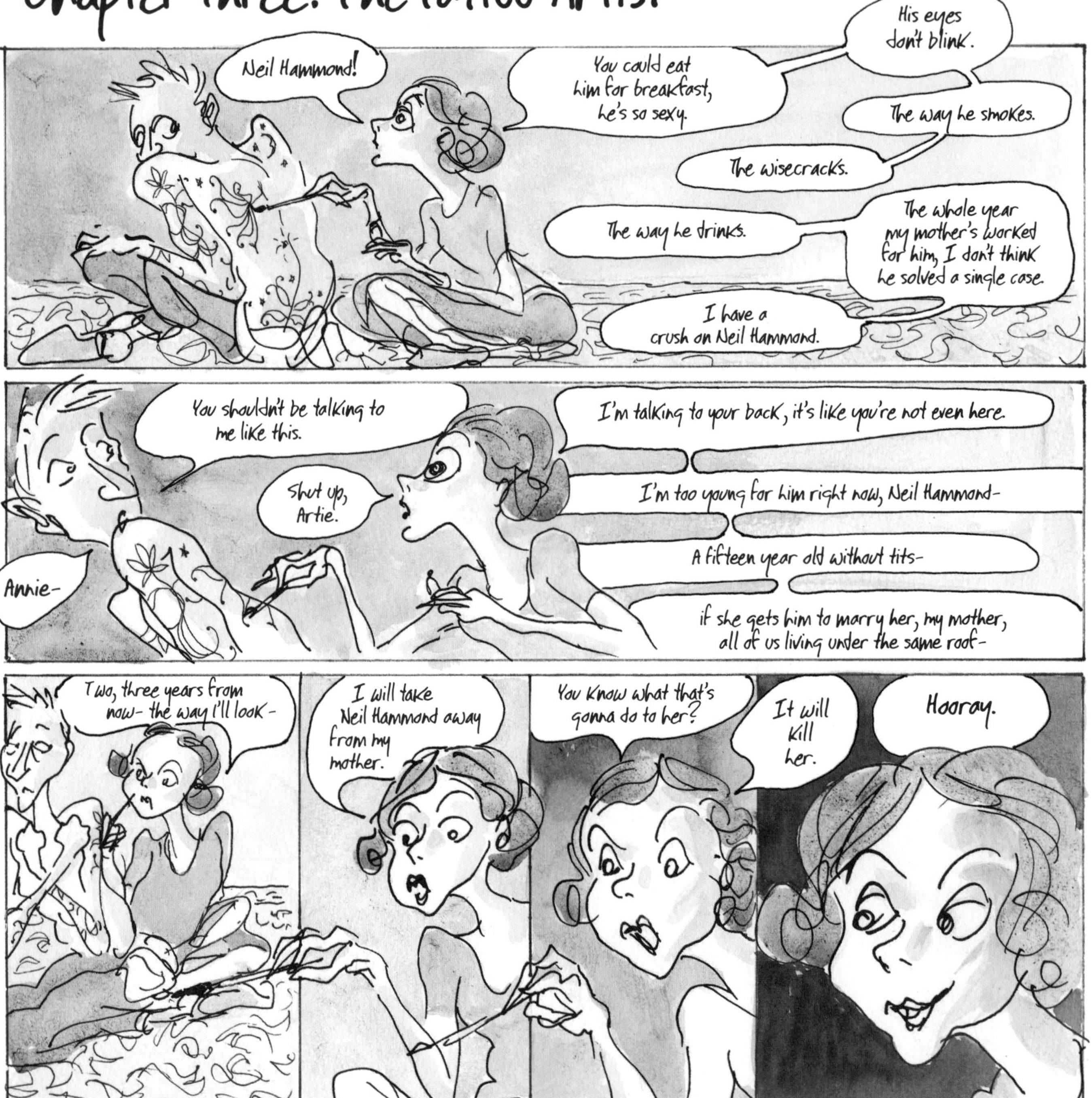
Neil Hammond!
You could eat him for breakfast, he's so sexy.
His eyes don't blink.
The way he smokes.
The wisecracks.
The way he drinks.
The whole year my mother's worked for him, I don't think he solved a single case.
I have a crush on Neil Hammond.
You shouldn't be talking to me like this.
Shut up, Artie.
Annie-
I'm talking to your back, it's like you're not even here.
I'm too young for him right now, Neil Hammond-
A fifteen year old without tits-
if she gets him to marry her, my mother, all of us living under the same roof-
Two, three years from now- the way I'll look-
I will take Neil Hammond away from my mother.
You Know what that's gonna do to her?
It will kill her.
Hooray.

Chapter Four: The Big Blonde

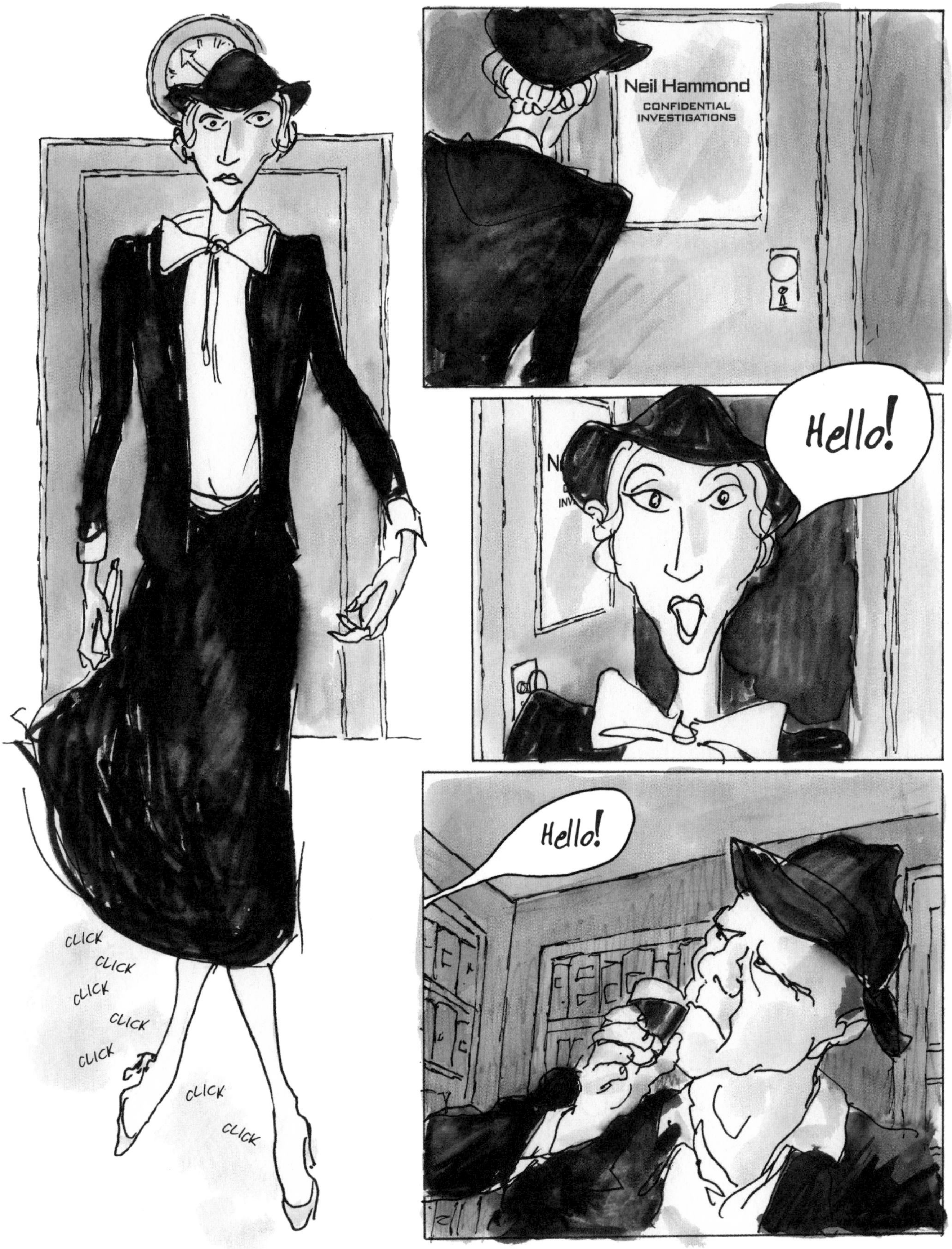
CLICK
CLICK
CLICK
CLICK
CLICK
CLICK
CLICK
Neil Hammond
CONFIDENTIAL
INVESTIGATIONS
Hello!
Hello!

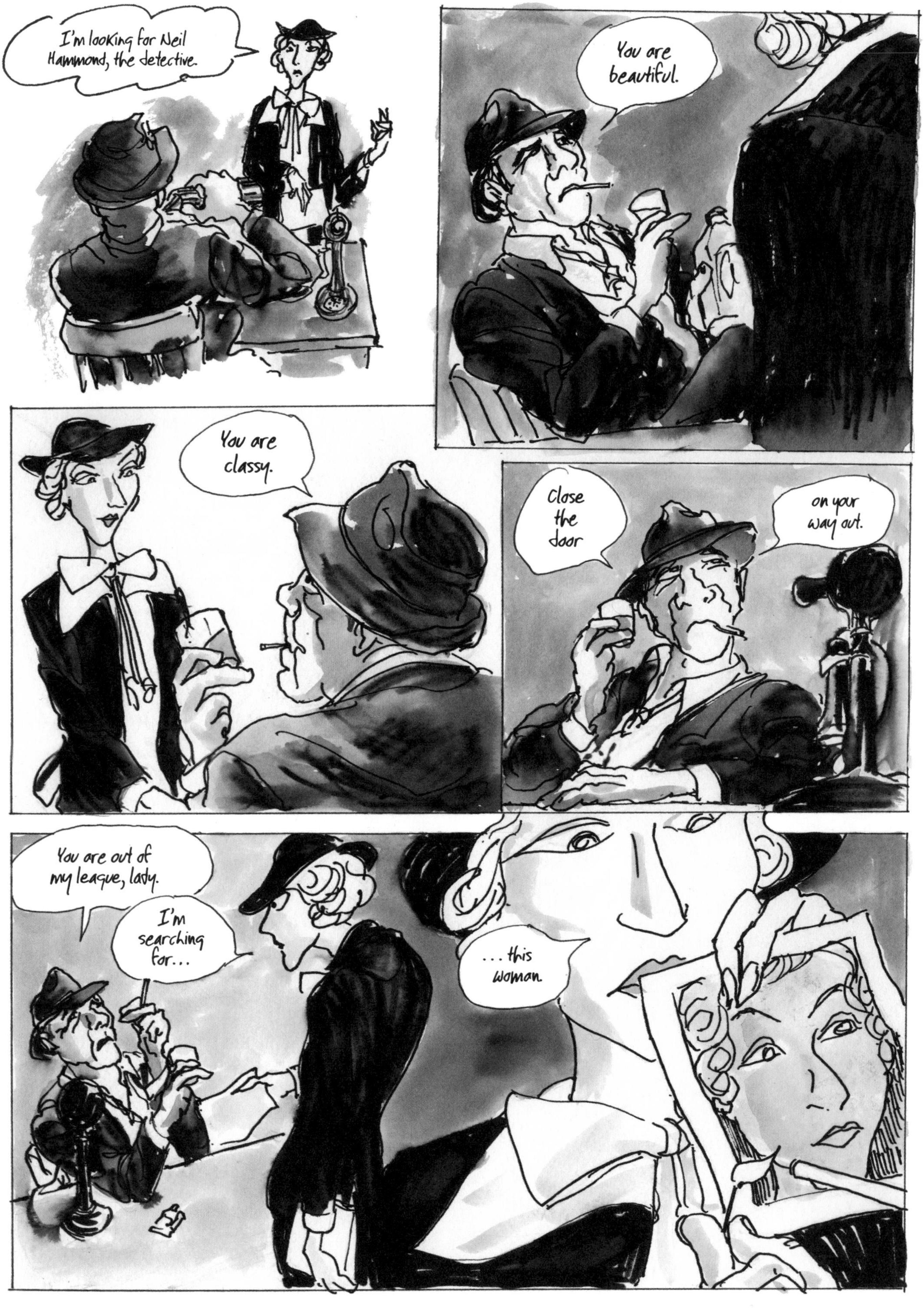
I'm looking for Neil Hammond, the detective.
You are beautiful.
You are classy.
Close the door
on your way out.
You are out of my league, lady.
I'm searching for...
... this woman.

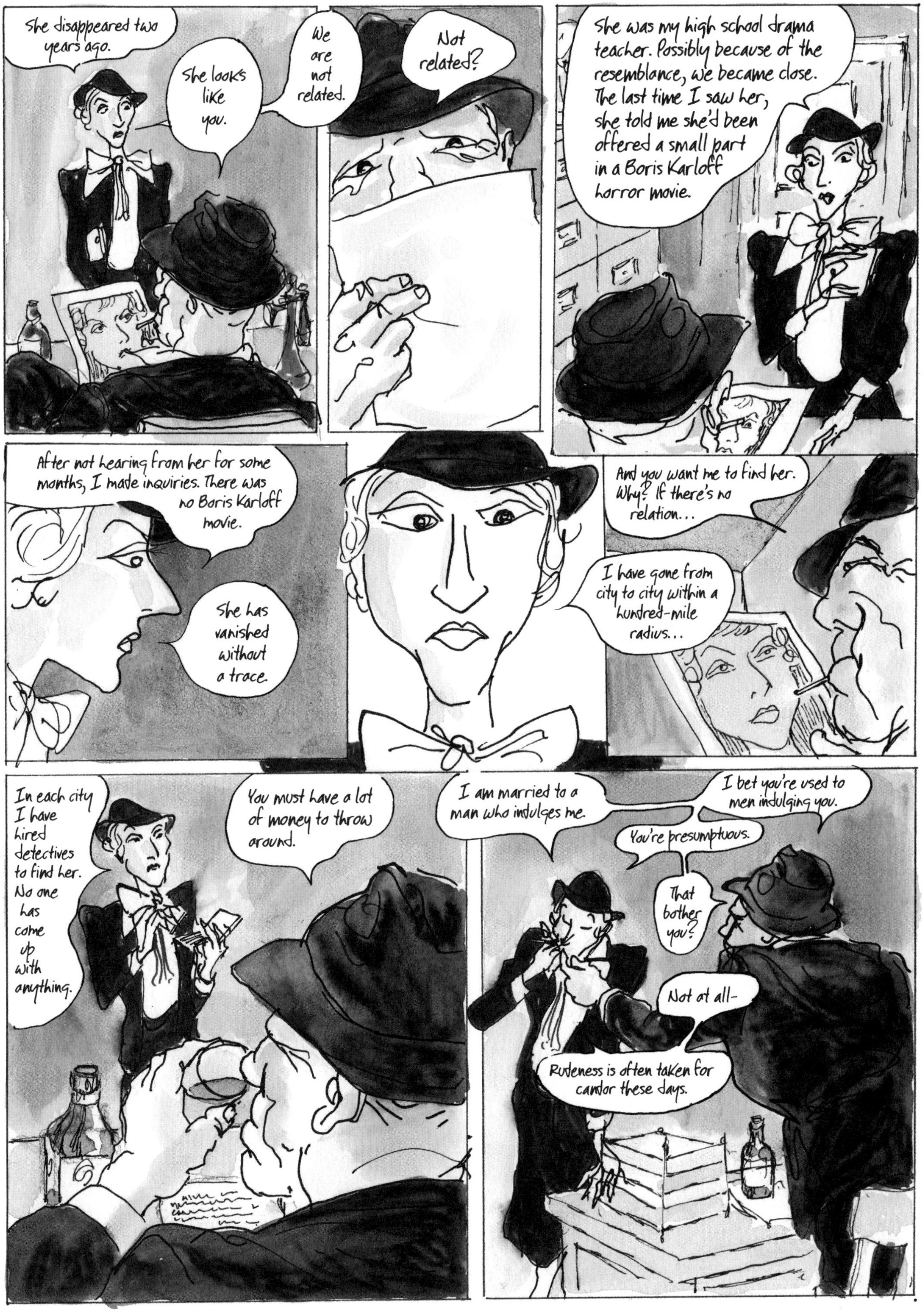
She disappeared two years ago.
She looks like you.
We are not related.
Not related?
She was my high school drama teacher. Possibly because of the resemblance, we became close. The last time I saw her, she told me she'd been offered a small part in a Boris Karloff horror movie.
After not hearing from her for some months, I made inquiries. There was no Boris Karloff movie.
She has vanished without a trace.
And you want me to find her. Why? If there's no relation...
I have gone from city to city within a hundred-mile radius...
In each city I have hired detectives to find her. No one has come up with anything.
You must have a lot of money to throw around.
I am married to a man who indulges me.
I bet you're used to men indulging you.
You're presumptuous.
That bother you?
Not at all-
Rudeness is often taken for candor these days.

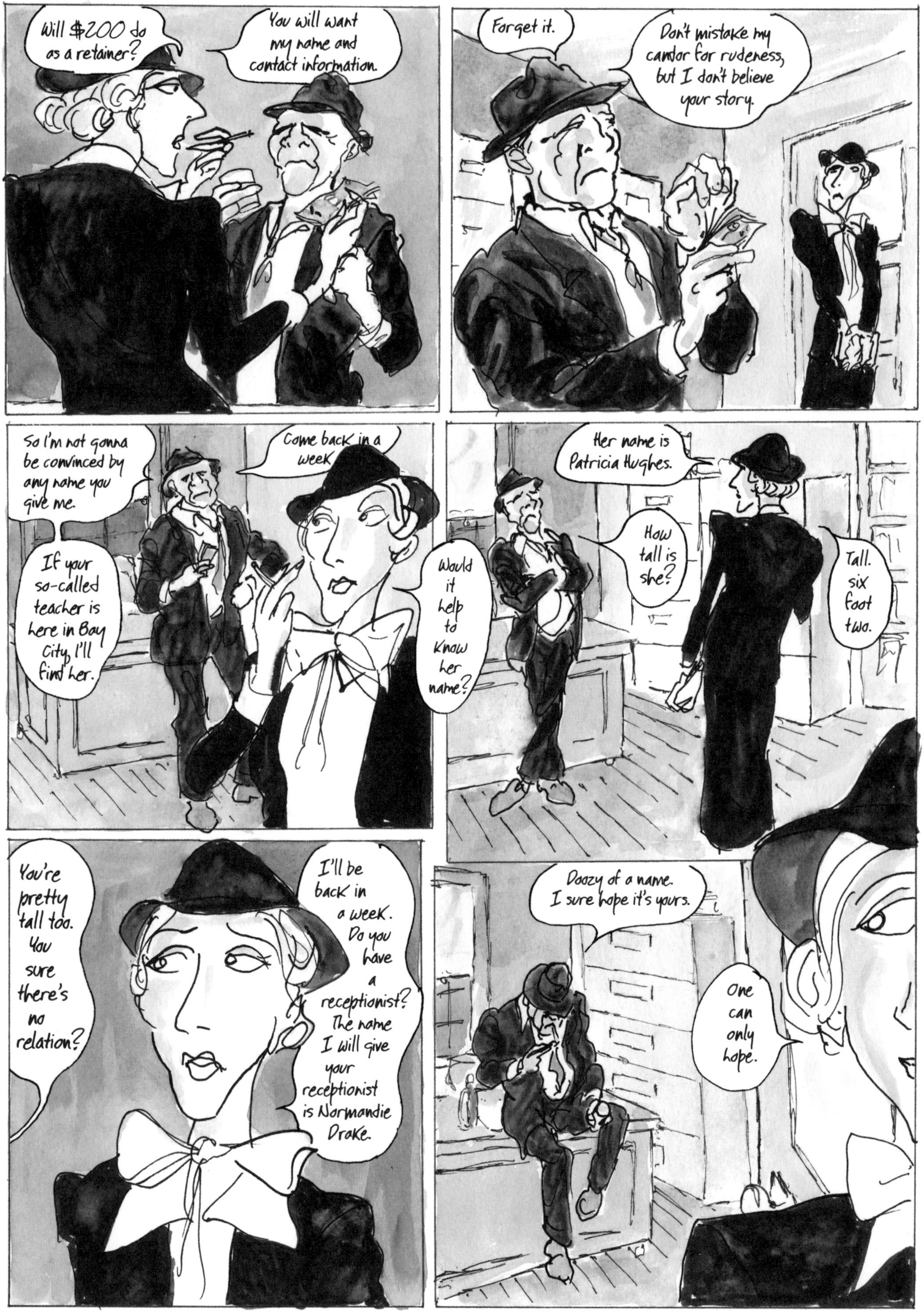
Will $200 do as a retainer?
You will want my name and contact information.
Forget it.
Don't mistake my candor for rudeness, but I don't believe your story.
So I'm not gonna be convinced by any name you give me.
If your so-called teacher is here in Bay City, I'll find her.
Come back in a week.
Would it help to know her name?
Her name is Patricia Hughes.
How tall is she?
Tall. six foot two.
You're pretty tall too. You sure there's no relation?
I'll be back in a week. Do you have a receptionist? The name I will give your receptionist is Normandie Drake.
Doozy of a name. I sure hope it's yours.
One can only hope.

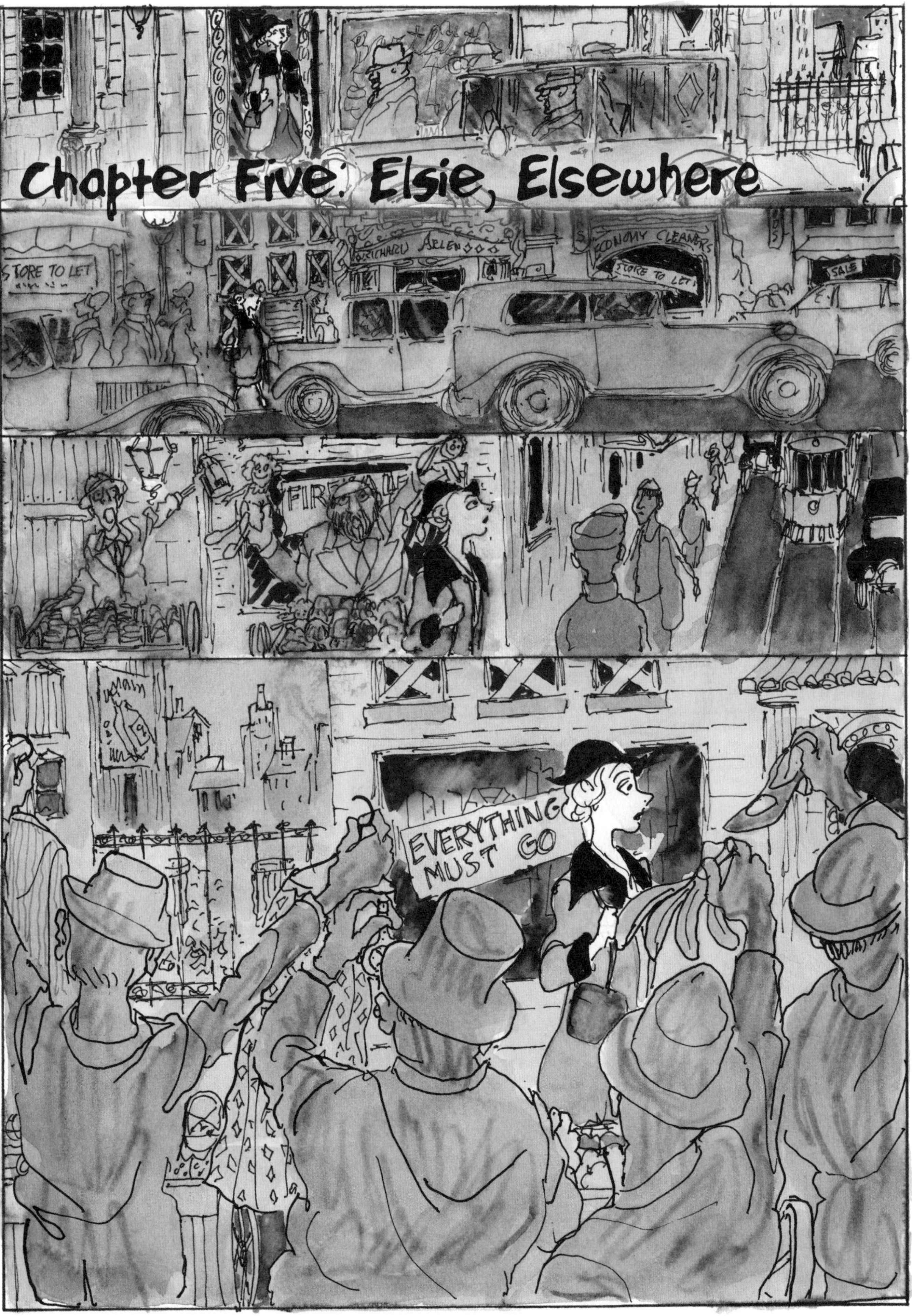
Chapter Five: Elsie, Elsewhere
STORE TO LET
RICHARD ARLEN
ECONOMY CLEANERS
STORE TO LET
SALE
EVERYTHING MUST GO

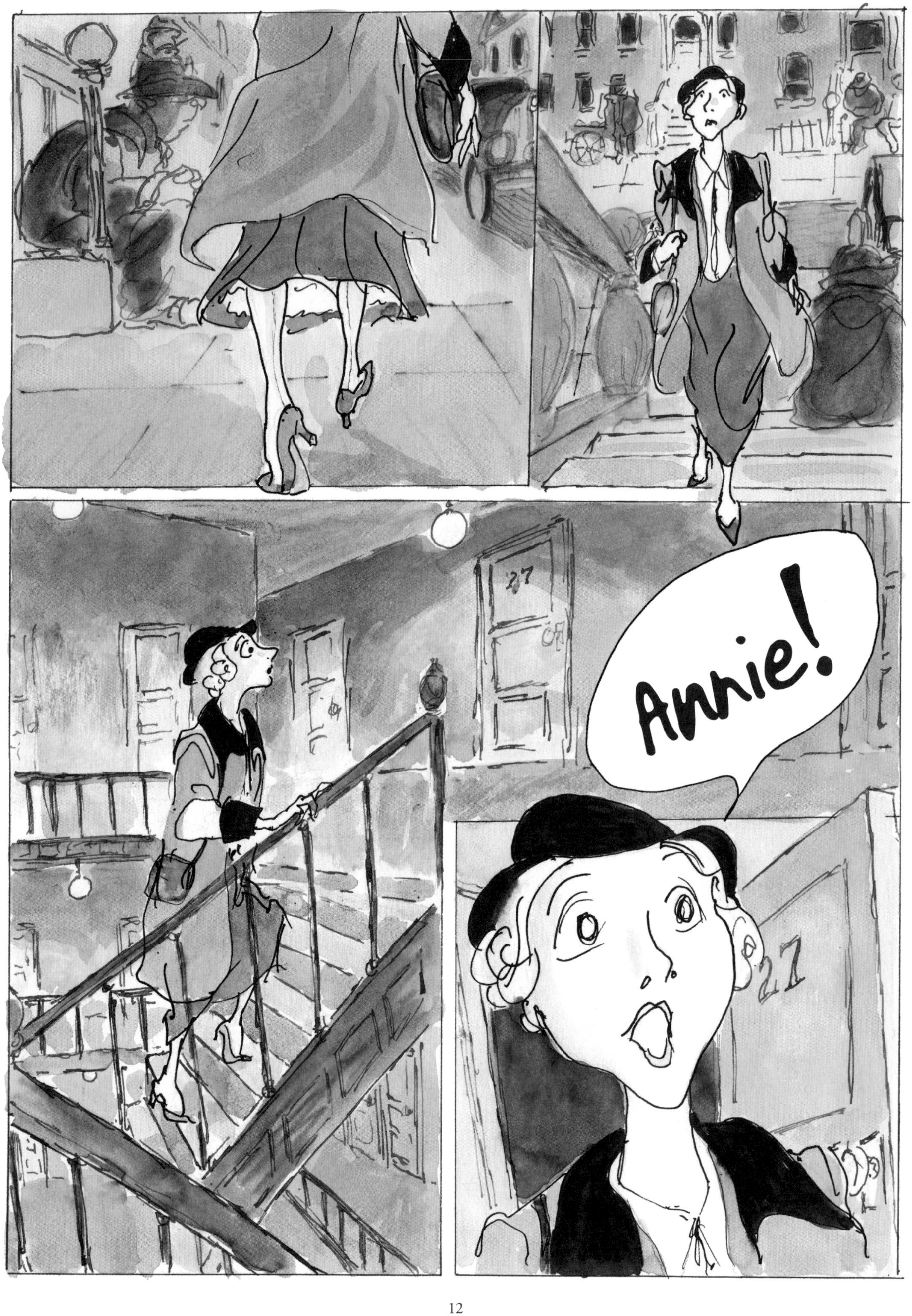
Annie!

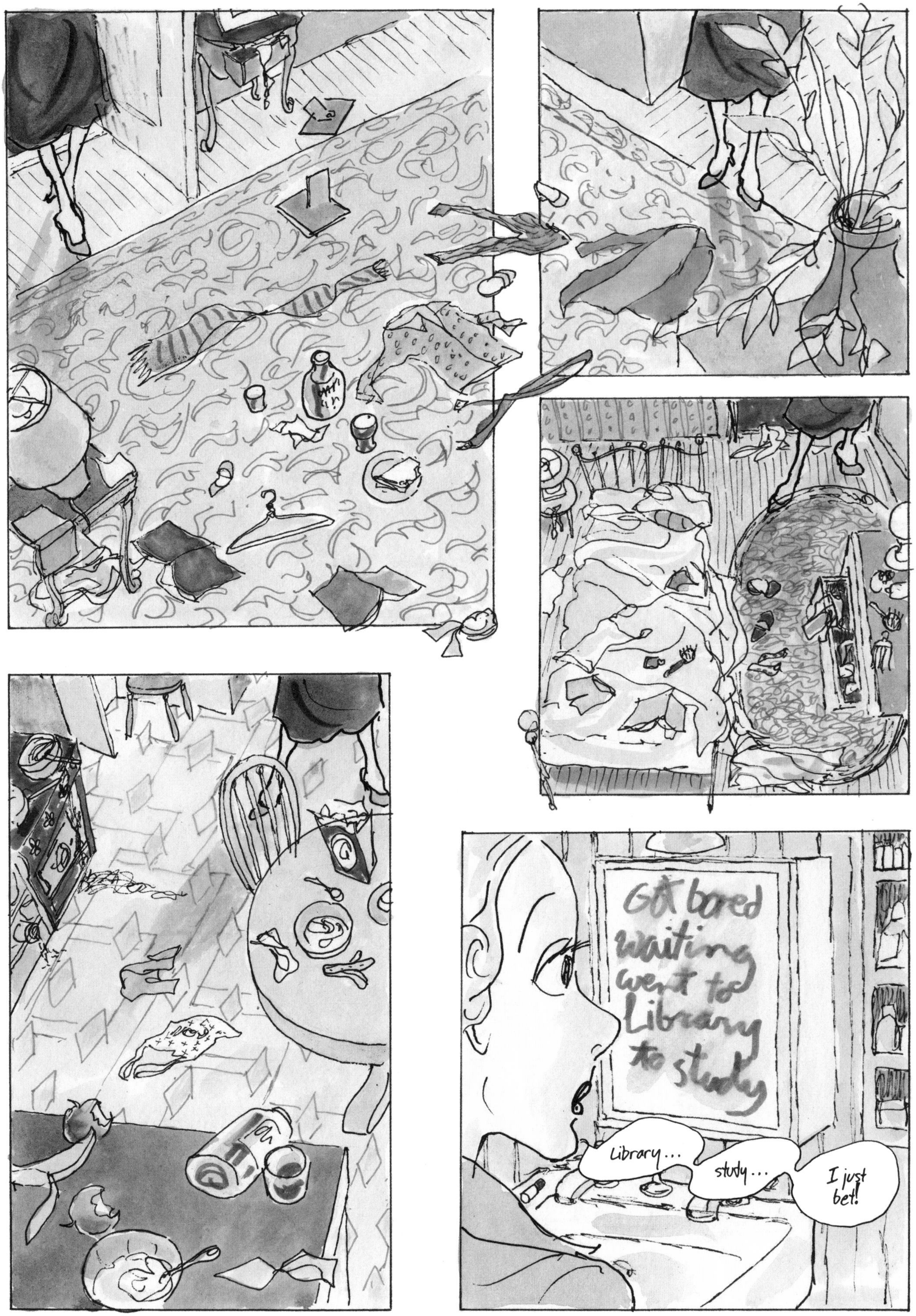
Got bored waiting went to Library to study
Library...
study...
I just bet!

Chapter Six: Shopping Spree

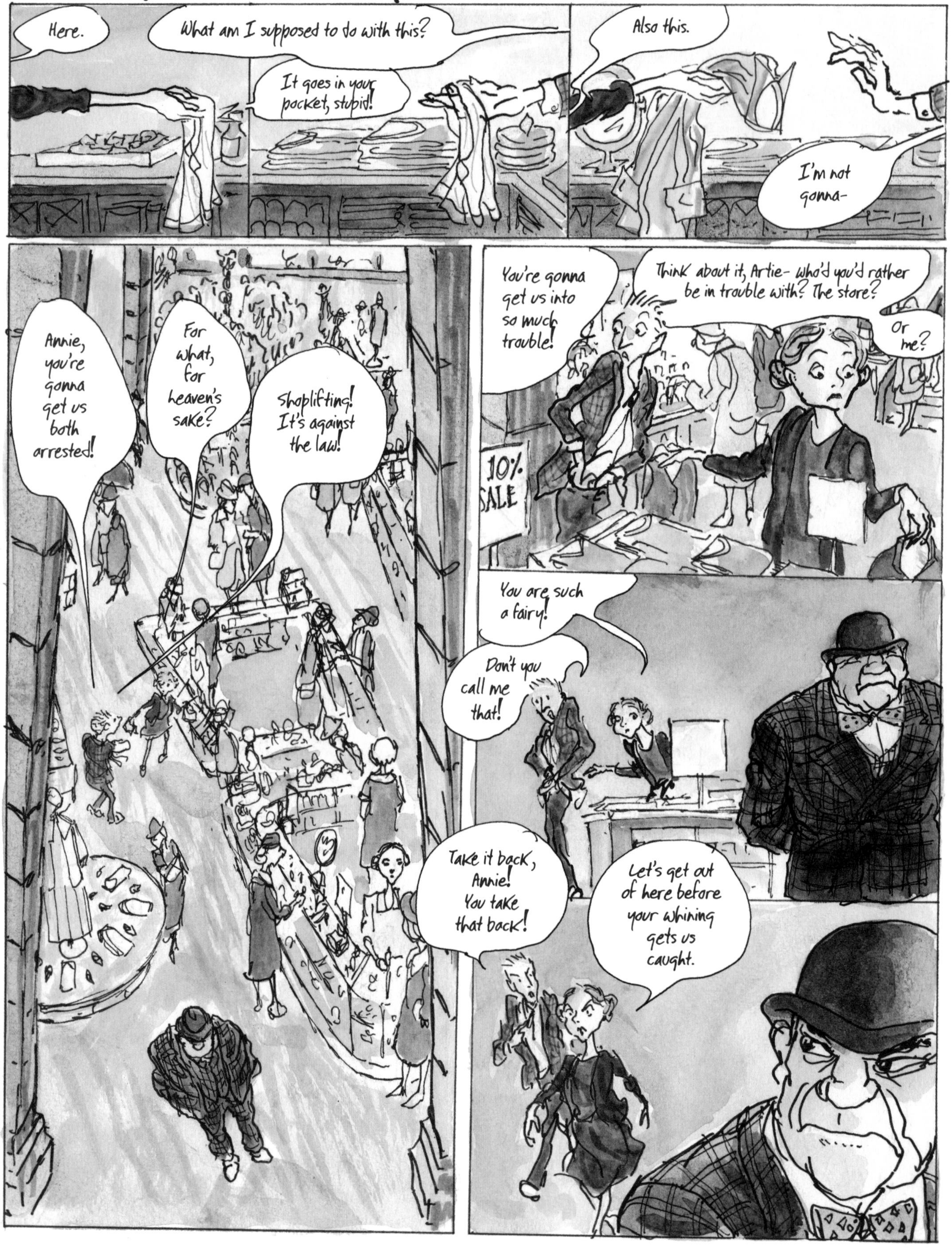
Here.
What am I supposed to do with this?
It goes in your pocket, stupid!
Also this.
I'm not gonna-
Annie, you're gonna get us both arrested!
For what, for heaven's sake?
Shoplifting! It's against the law!
You're gonna get us into so much trouble!
Think about it, Artie- who'd you'd rather be in trouble with? The store?
Or me?
10% SALE
You are such a fairy!
Don't you call me that!
Take it back, Annie! You take that back!
Let's get out of here before your whining gets us caught.

Chapter Seven: The Come-On

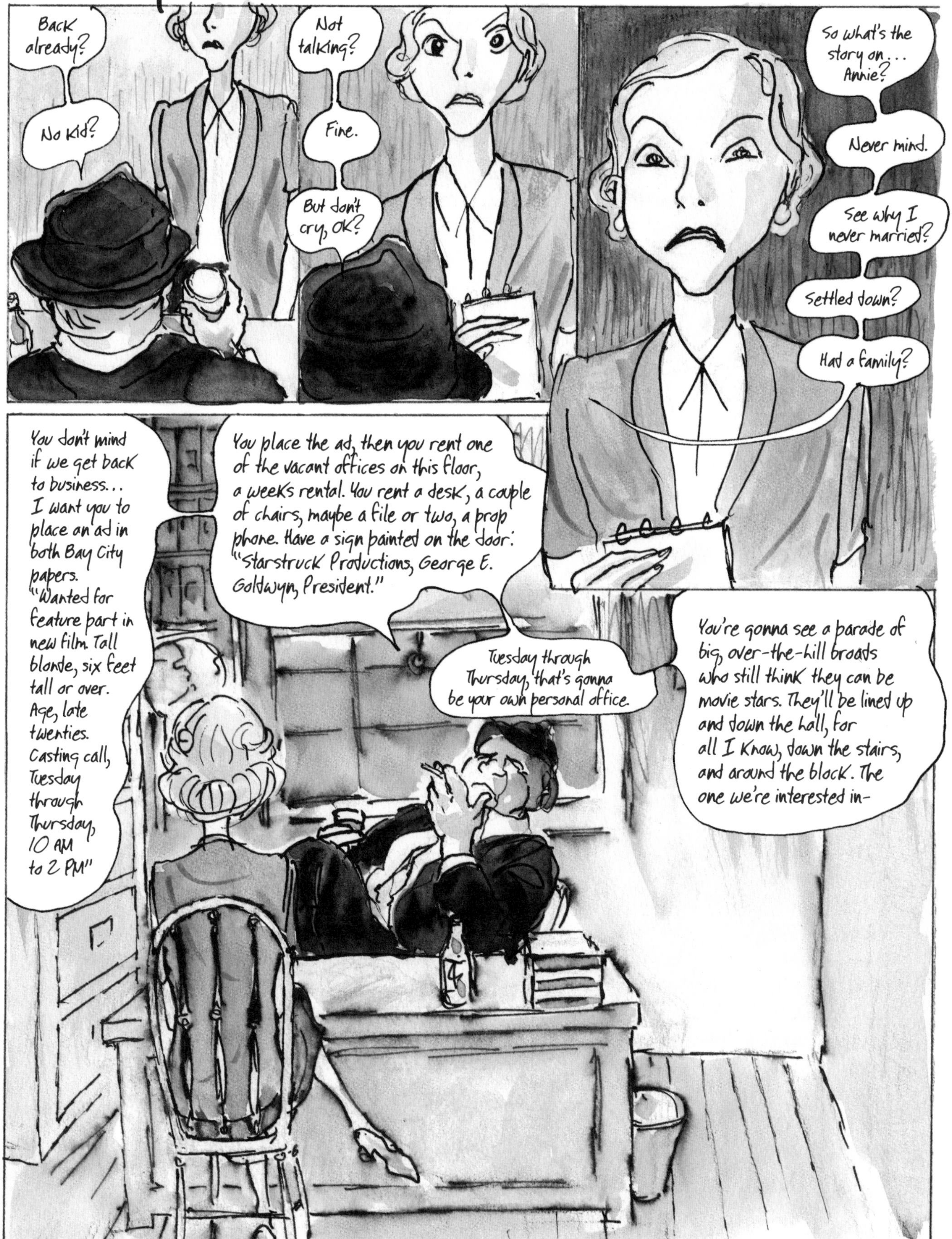

Back already?
No kid?
Not talking?
Fine.
But don't cry, OK?
So what's the story on... Annie?
Never mind.
See why I never married?
Settled down?
Had a family?
You don't mind if we get back to business... I want you to place an ad in both Bay City papers. "Wanted for feature part in new film. Tall blonde, six feet tall or over. Age, late twenties. Casting call, Tuesday through Thursday, 10 AM to 2 PM"
You place the ad, then you rent one of the vacant offices on this floor, a weeks rental. You rent a desk, a couple of chairs, maybe a file or two, a prop phone. Have a sign painted on the door: "Starstruck Productions, George E. Goldwyn, President."
Tuesday through Thursday, that's gonna be your own personal office.
You're gonna see a parade of big, over-the-hill broads who still think they can be movie stars. They'll be lined up and down the hall, for all I know, down the stairs, and around the block. The one we're interested in-

Chapter Eight: On the Run

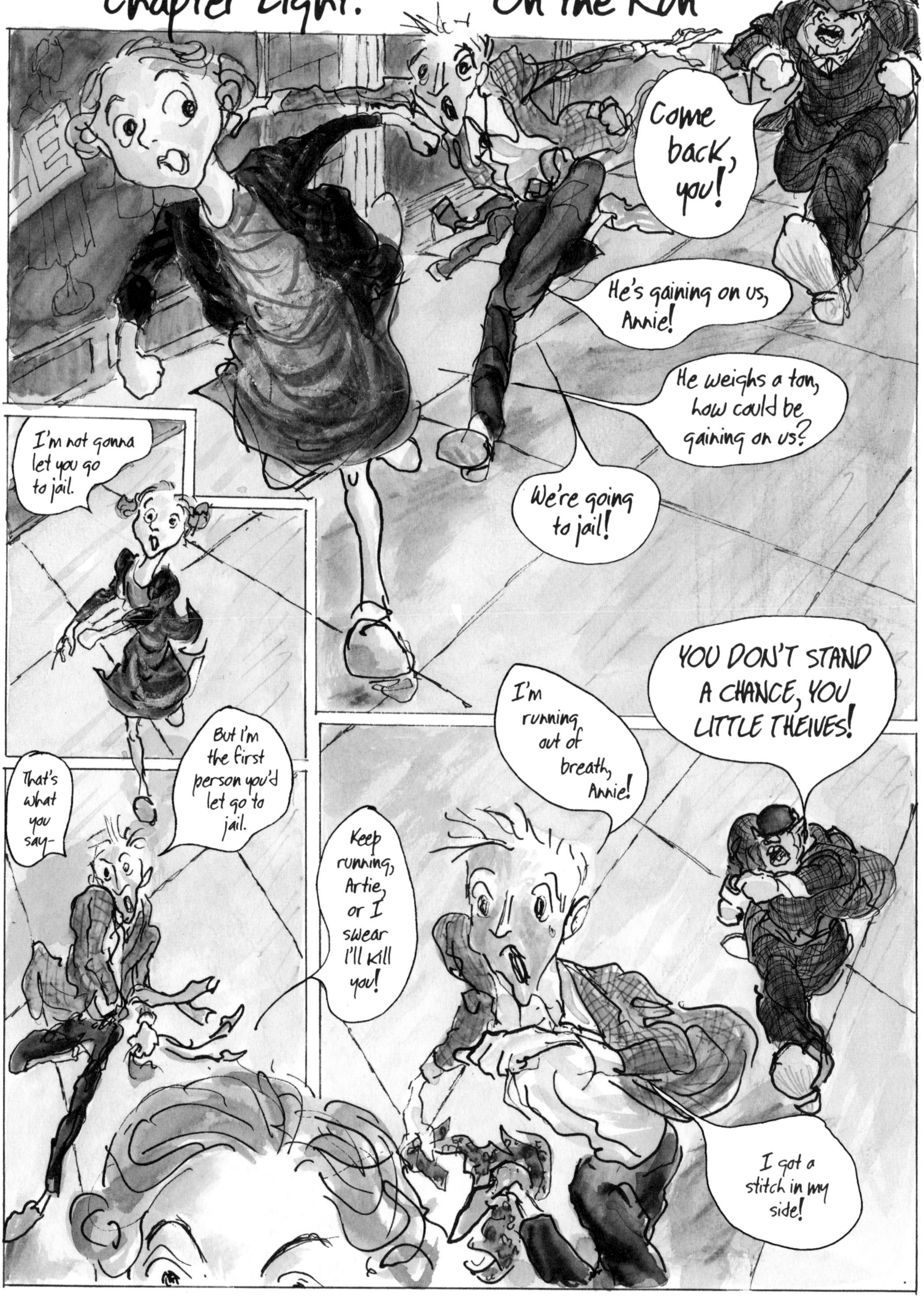
Come back, you!
He's gaining on us, Annie!
He weighs a ton, how could be gaining on us?
We're going to jail!
I'm not gonna let you go to jail.
That's what you say-
But I'm the first person you'd let go to jail.
Keep running, Artie, or I swear I'll kill you!
I'm running out of breath, Annie!
YOU DON'T STAND A CHANCE, YOU LITTLE THEIVES!
I got a stitch in my side!

Chapter Nine: Gotcha!

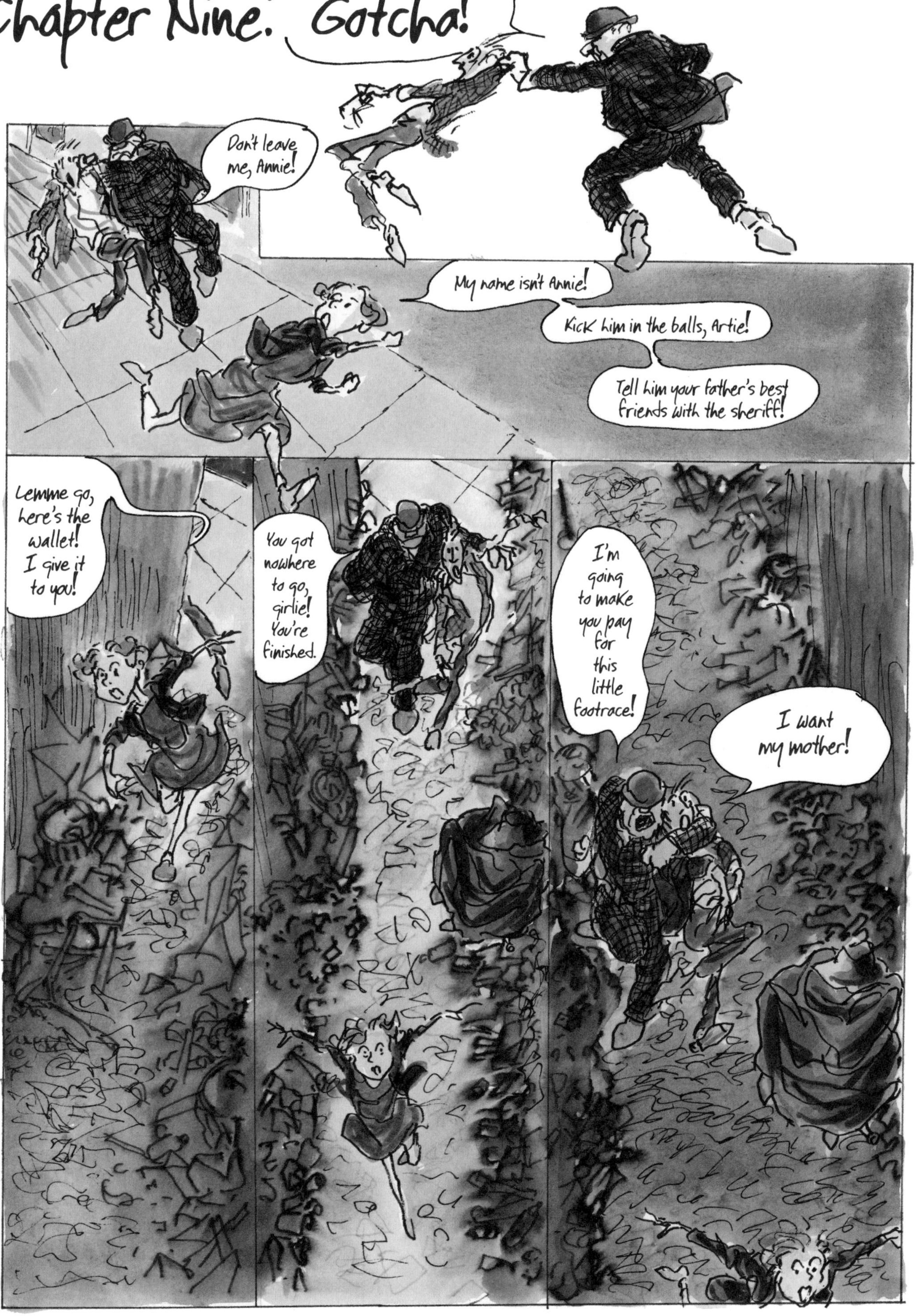
Don't leave me, Annie!
My name isn't Annie!
Kick him in the balls, Artie!
Tell him your father's best friends with the sheriff!
Lemme go, here's the wallet! I give it to you!
You got nowhere to go, girlie! You're finished.
I'm going to make you pay for this little footrace!
I want my mother!

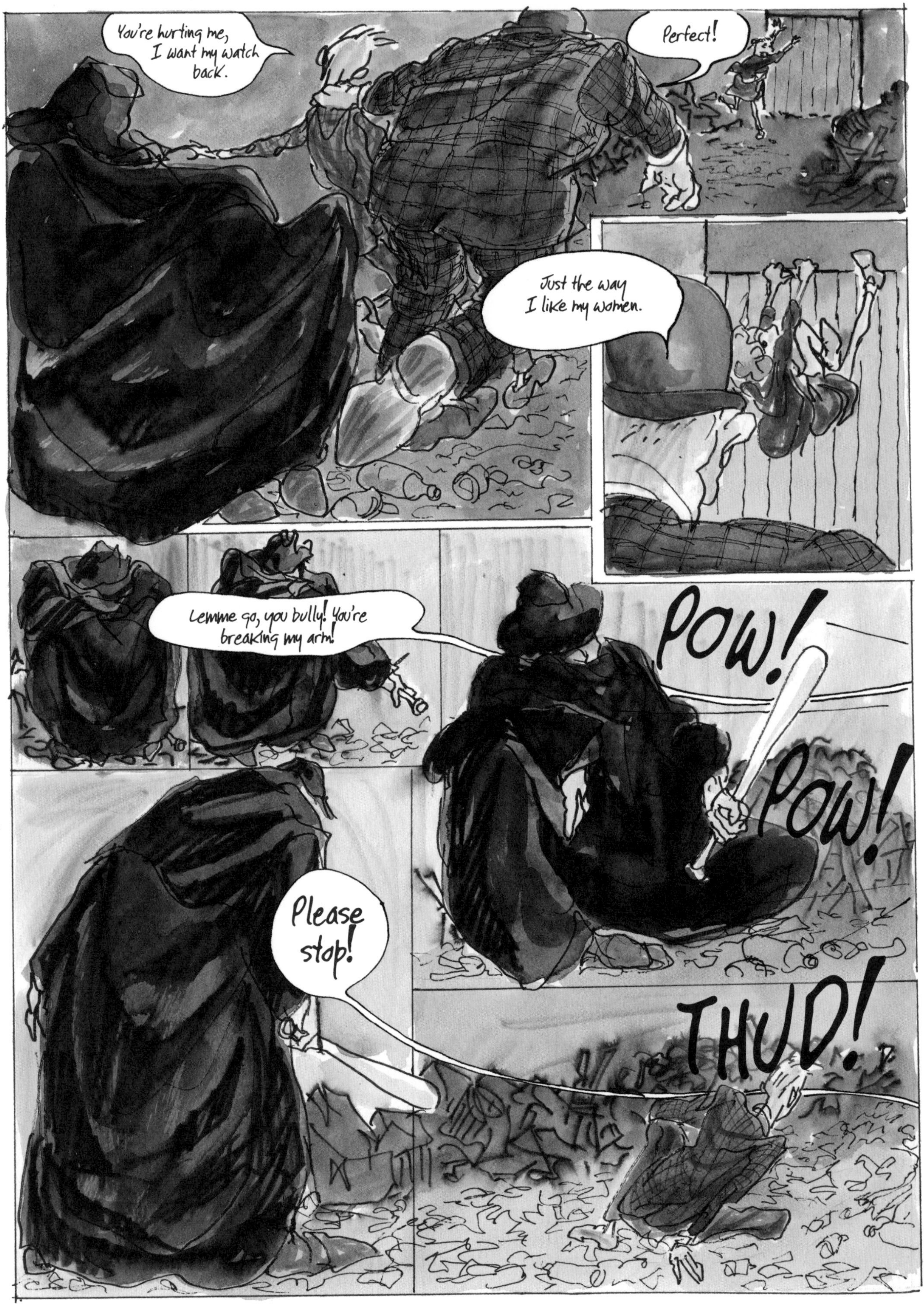
You're hurting me, I want my watch back.
Perfect!
Just the way I like my women.
Lemme go, you bully! You're breaking my arm!
POW!
POW!
Please stop!
THUD!

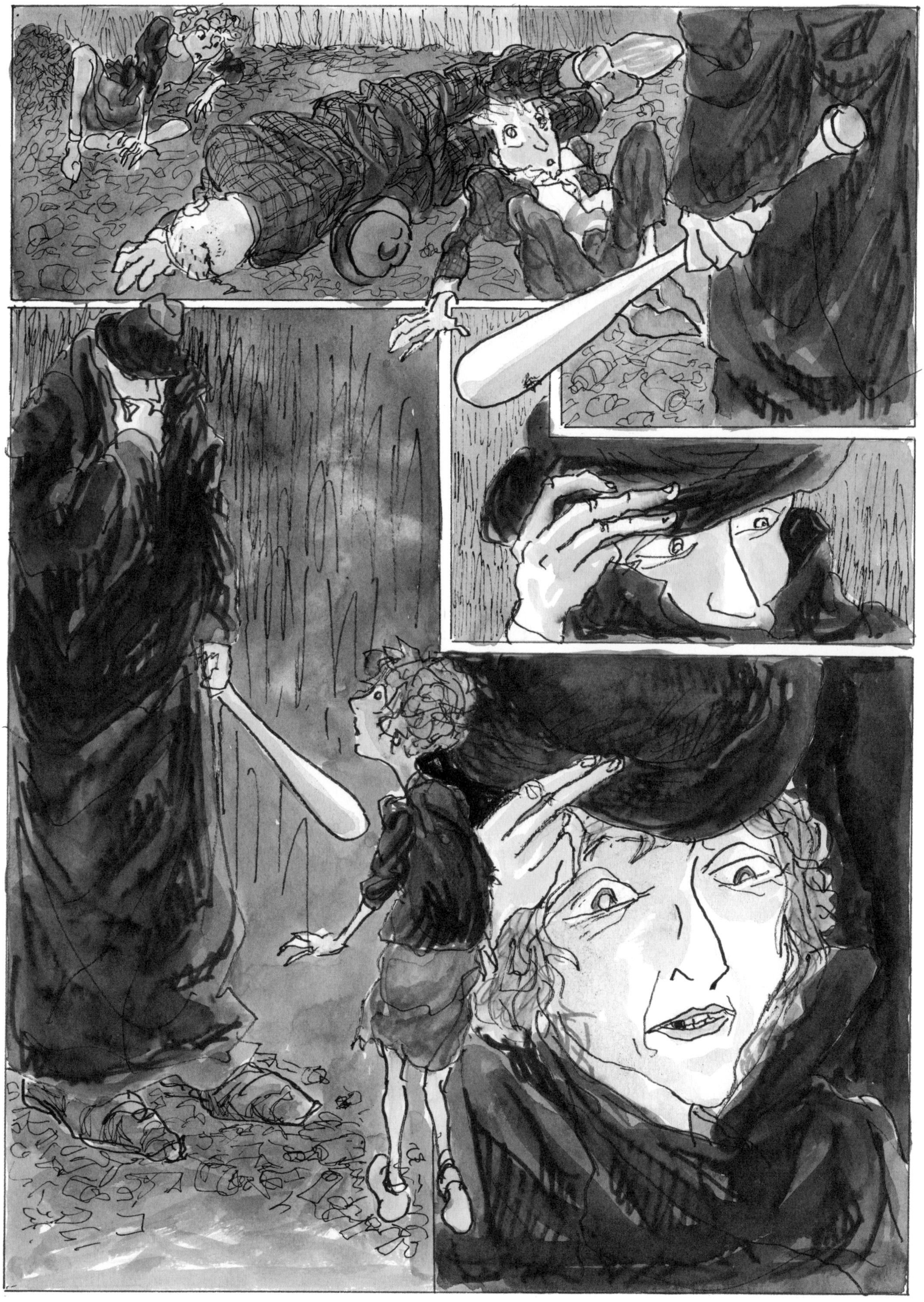

Chapter Ten: The Invite

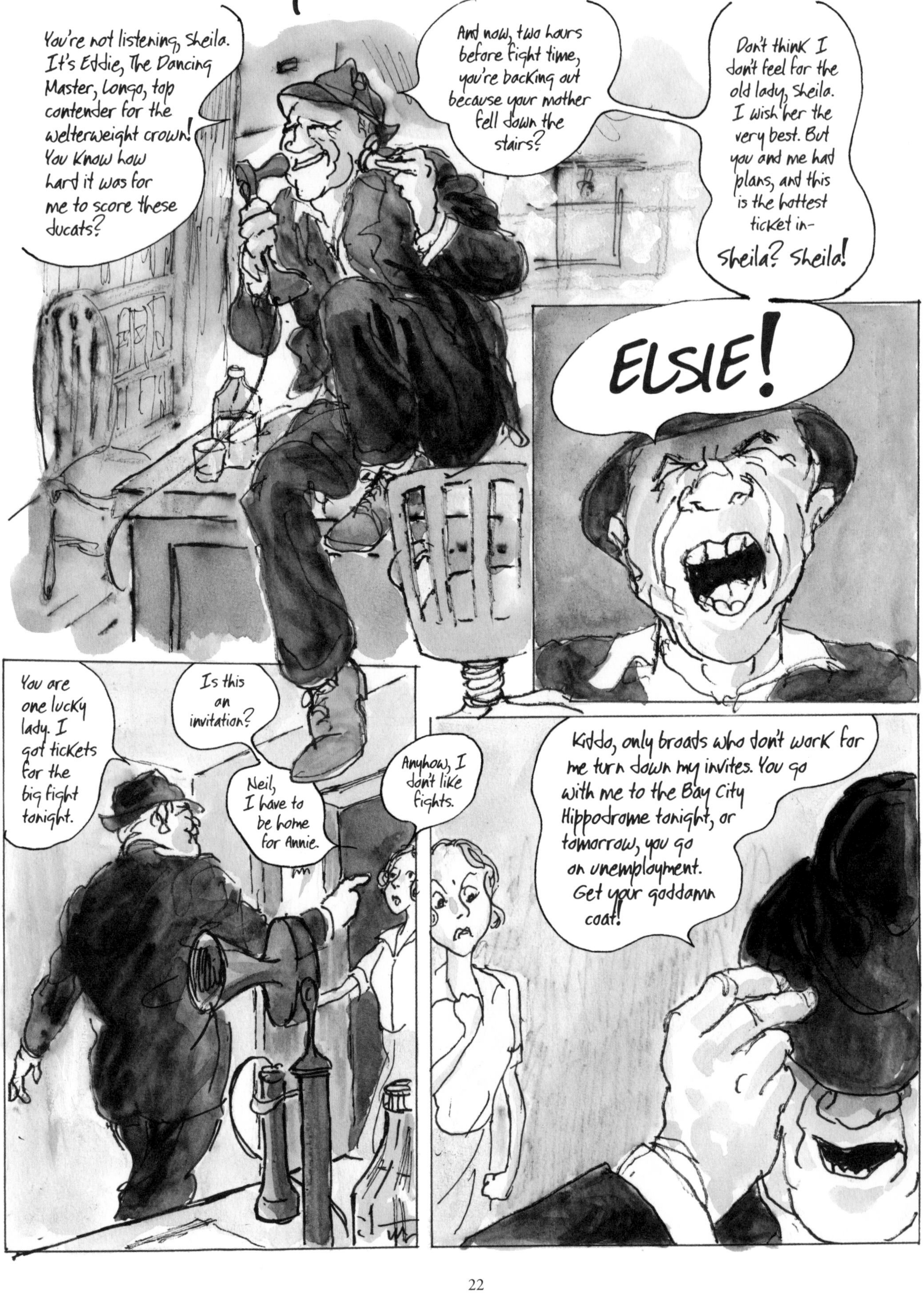

You're not listening, Sheila. It's Eddie, The Dancing Master, Longo, top contender for the welterweight crown! You know how hard it was for me to score these ducats?
And now, two hours before fight time, you're backing out because your mother fell down the stairs?
Don't think I don't feel for the old lady, Sheila. I wish her the very best. But you and me had plans, and this is the hottest ticket in- Sheila? Sheila!
ELSIE!
You are one lucky lady. I got tickets for the big fight tonight.
Is this an invitation?
Neil, I have to be home for Annie.
Anyhow, I don't like fights.
Kiddo, only broads who don't work for me turn down my invites. You go with me to the Bay City Hippodrome tonight, or tomorrow, you go on unemployment. Get your goddamn coat!

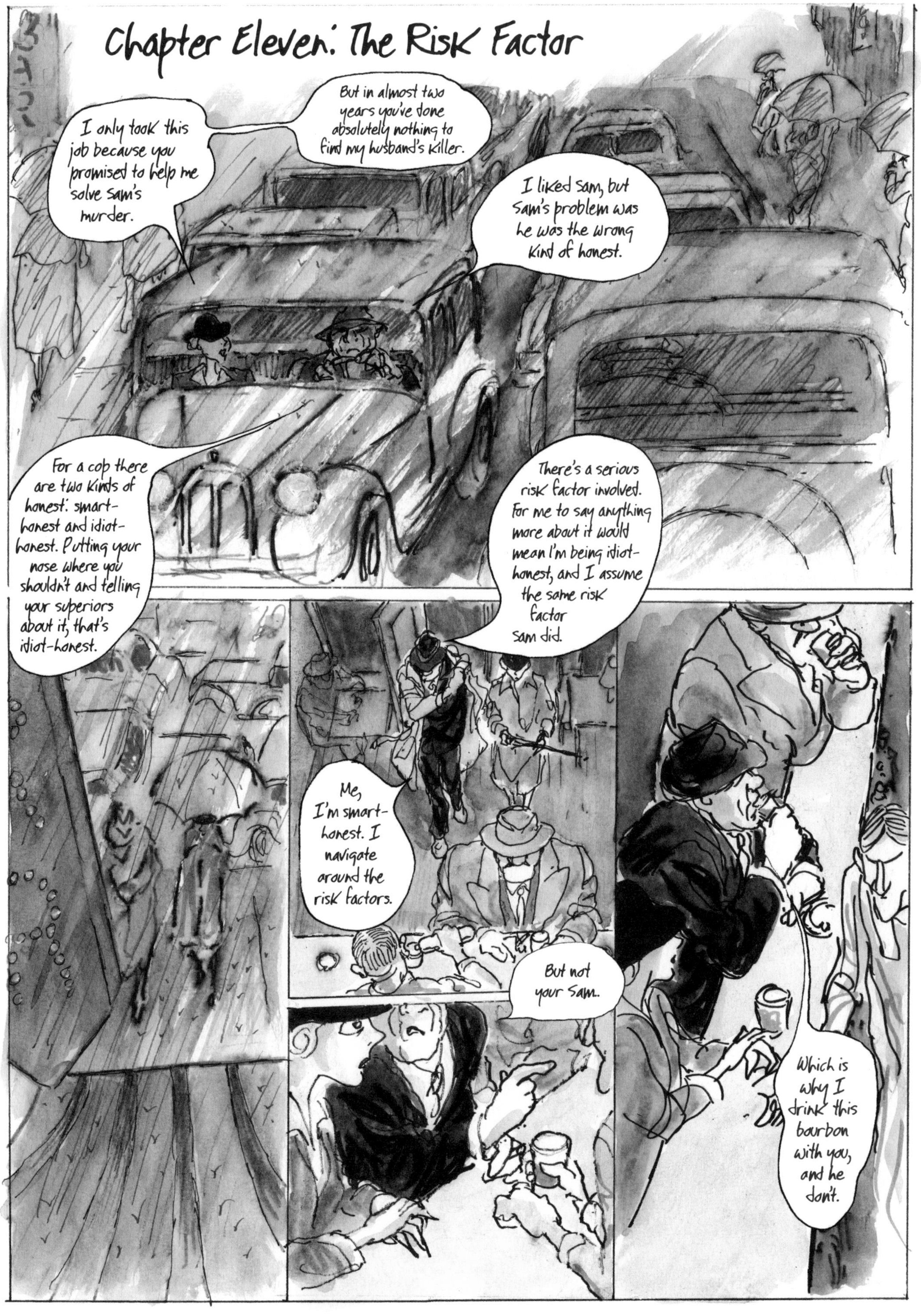
Chapter Eleven: The Risk Factor
I only took this job because you promised to help me solve Sam's murder.
But in almost two years you've done absolutely nothing to find my husband's killer.
I liked Sam, but Sam's problem was he was the wrong kind of honest.
For a cop there are two kinds of honest: smart-honest and idiot-honest. Putting your nose where you shouldn't and telling your superiors about it, that's idiot-honest.
There's a serious risk factor involved. For me to say anything more about it would mean I'm being idiot-honest, and I assume the same risk factor Sam did.
Me, I'm smart-honest. I navigate around the risk factors.
But not your Sam.
Which is why I drink this bourbon with you, and he don't.

24

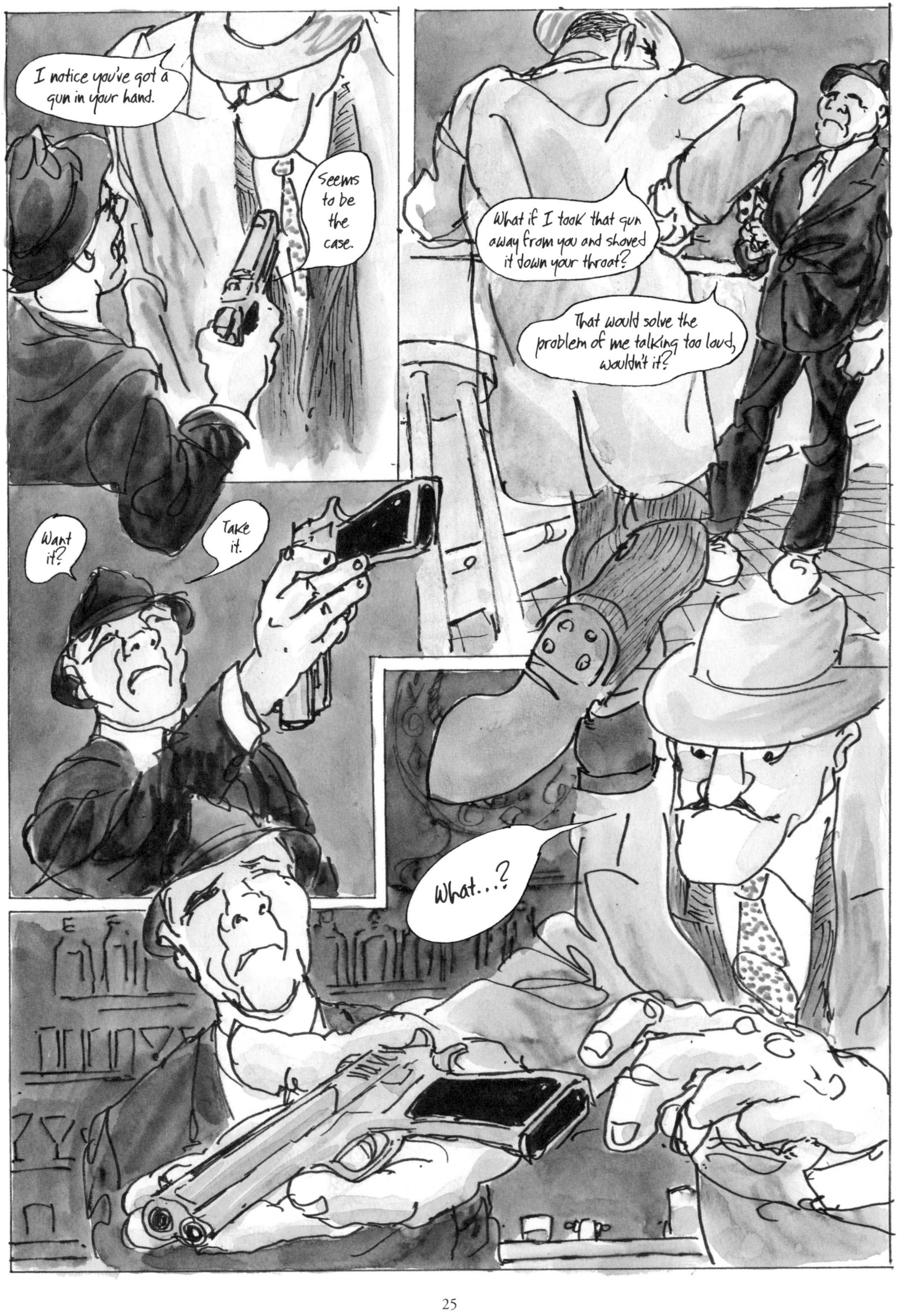
I notice you've got a gun in your hand.
Seems to be the case.
What if I took that gun away from you and shoved it down your throat?
That would solve the problem of me talking too loud, wouldn't it?
Want it?
Take it.
What...?

Chapter Twelve: The Tall Woman

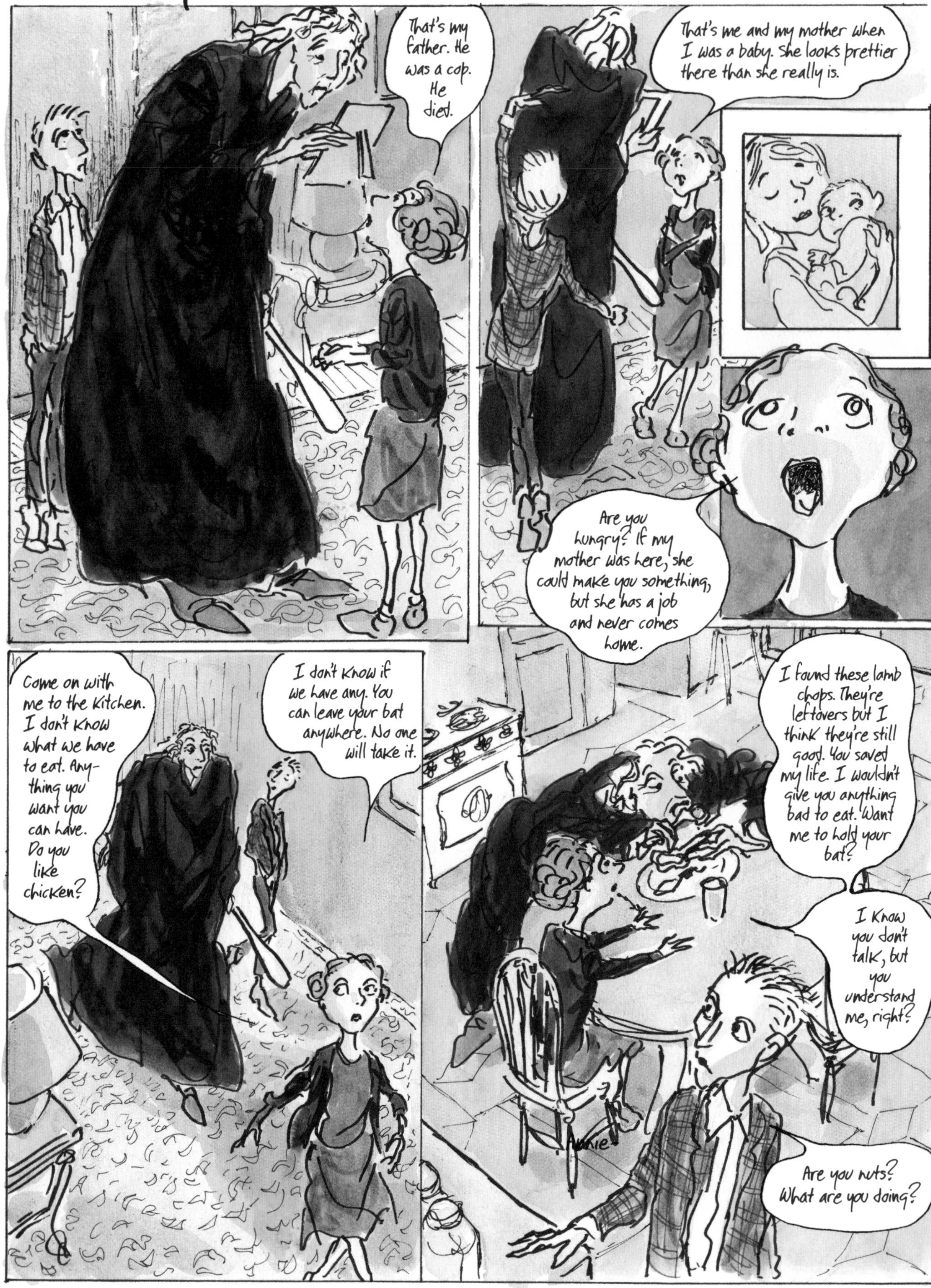
That's my father. He was a cop. He died.
That's me and my mother when I was a baby. She looks prettier there than she really is.
Are you hungry? If my mother was here, she could make you something, but she has a job and never comes home.
Come on with me to the kitchen. I don't know what we have to eat. Any-thing you want you can have. Do you like chicken?
I don't know if we have any. You can leave your bat anywhere. No one will take it.
I found these lamb chops. They're leftovers but I think they're still good. You saved my life. I wouldn't give you anything bad to eat. Want me to hold your bat?
I know you don't talk, but you understand me, right?
Are you nuts? What are you doing?

Chapter Thirteen: The Dancing Master

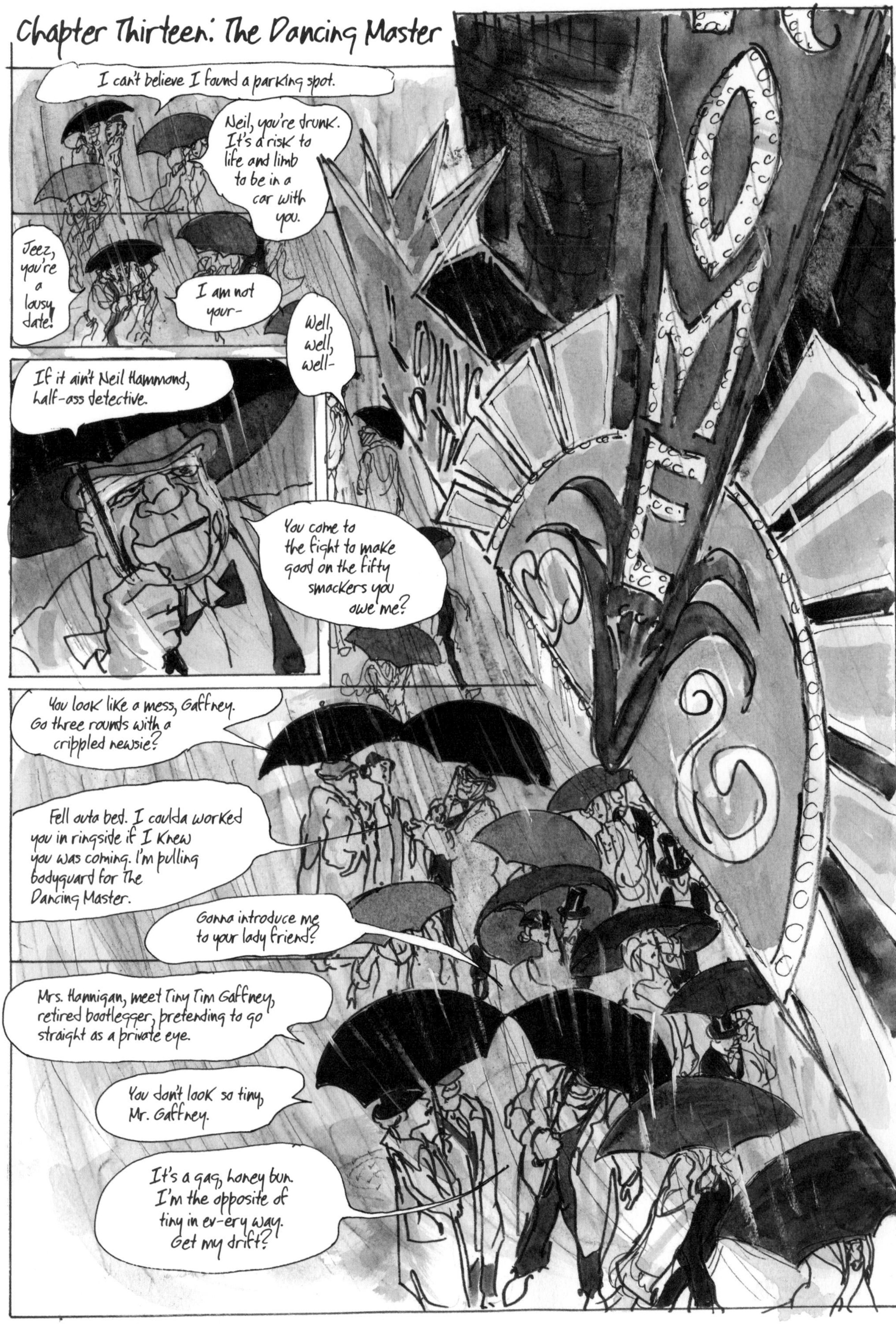

I can't believe I found a parking spot.
Neil, you're drunk. It's a risk to life and limb to be in a car with you.
Jeez, you're a lousy date!
I am not your-
Well, well, well-
If it ain't Neil Hammond, half-ass detective.
You come to the fight to make good on the fifty smackers you owe me?
You look like a mess, Gaffney. Go three rounds with a crippled newsie?
Fell outa bed. I coulda worked you in ringside if I knew you was coming. I'm pulling bodyguard for The Dancing Master.
Gonna introduce me to your lady friend?
Mrs. Hannigan, meet Tiny Tim Gaffney, retired bootlegger, pretending to go straight as a private eye.
You don't look so tiny, Mr. Gaffney.
It's a gag, honey bun. I'm the opposite of tiny in ev-ery way. Get my drift?

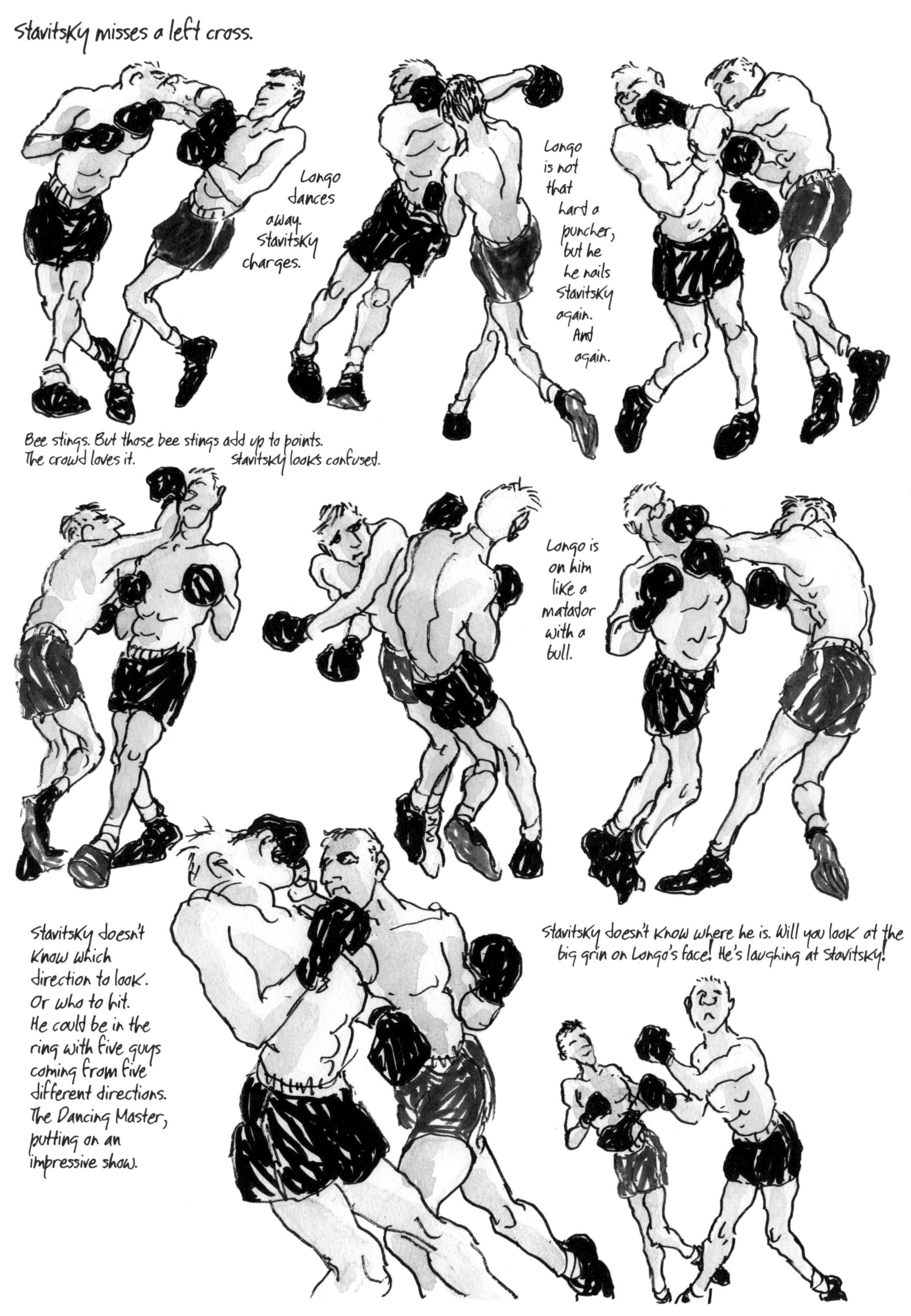
Stavitsky misses a left cross.
Longo dances away. Stavitsky charges.
Longo is not that hard a puncher, but he he nails Stavitsky again. And again.
Bee stings. But those bee stings add up to points. The crowd loves it.
Stavitsky looks confused.
Longo is on him like a matador with a bull.
Stavitsky doesn't know which direction to look. Or who to hit. He could be in the ring with five guys coming from five different directions. The Dancing Master, putting on an impressive show.
Stavitsky doesn't know where he is. Will you look at the big grin on Longo's face! He's laughing at Stavitsky!

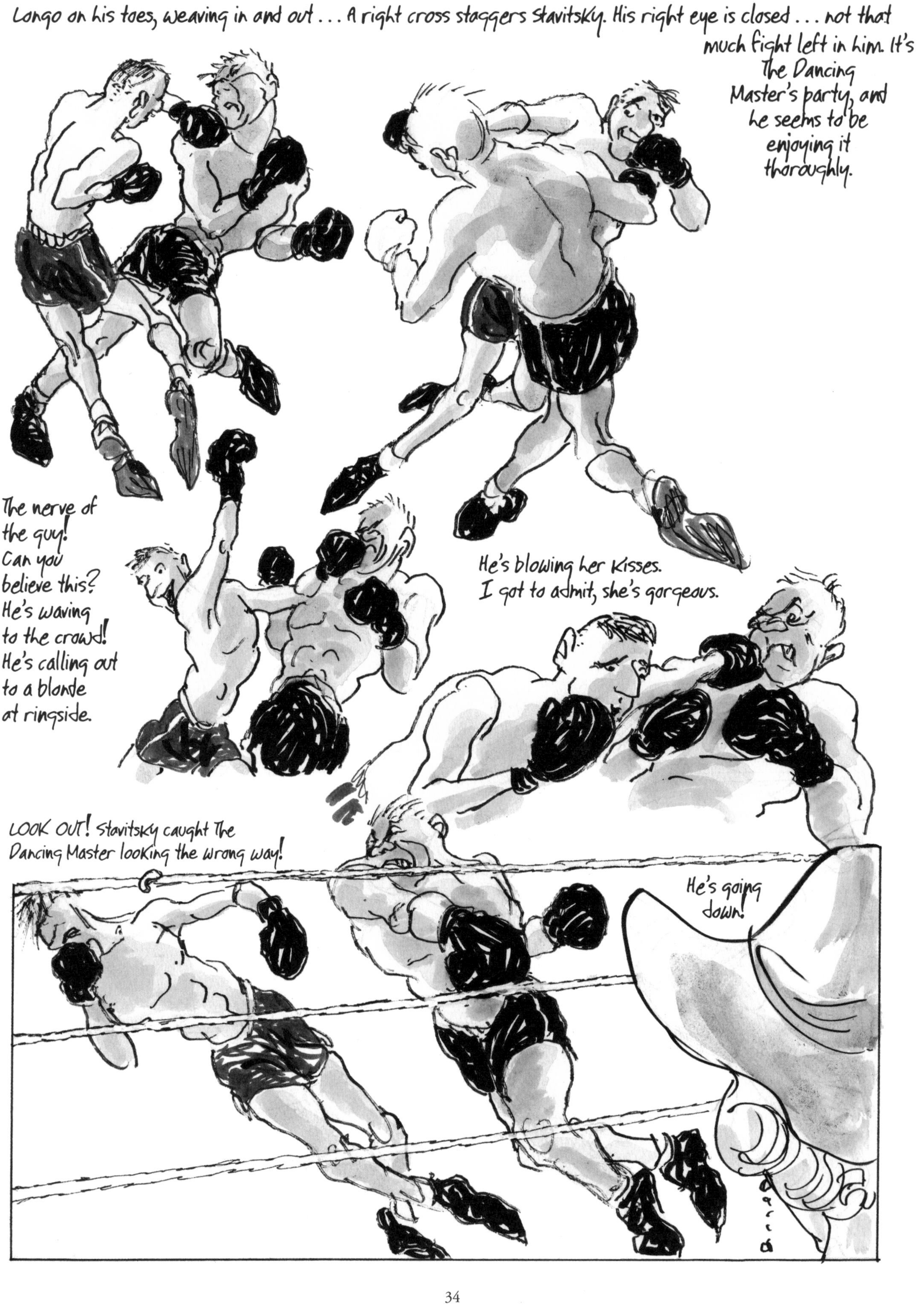
Longo on his toes, weaving in and out . . . A right cross staggers Stavitsky. His right eye is closed . . . not that much fight left in him. It's The Dancing Master's party, and he seems to be enjoying it thoroughly.
The nerve of the guy! Can you believe this? He's waving to the crowd! He's calling out to a blonde at ringside.
He's blowing her kisses. I got to admit, she's gorgeous.
LOOK OUT! Stavitsky caught The Dancing Master looking the wrong way!
He's going down!

Chapter Fourteen: Vacancy

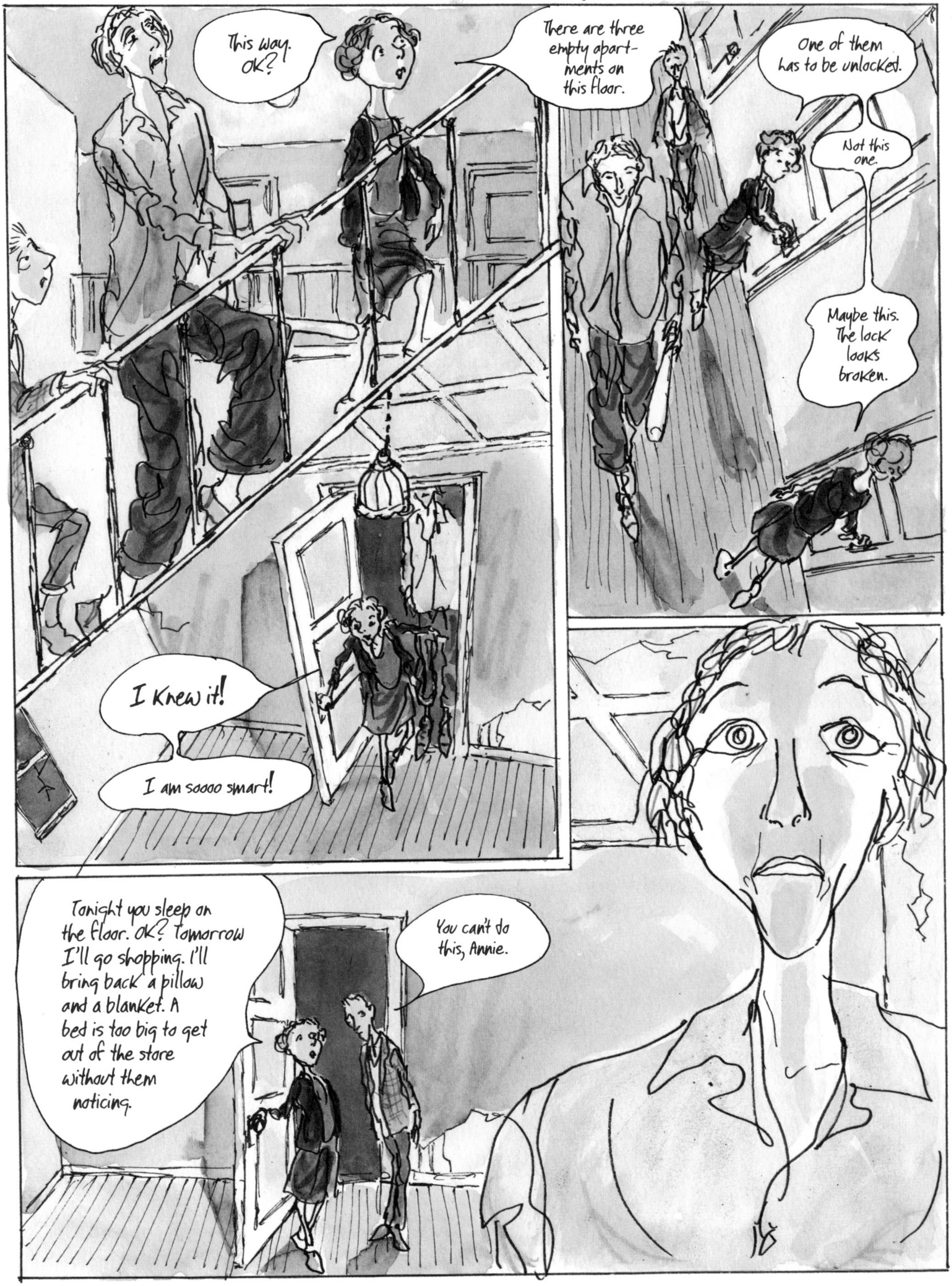
This way. OK?
There are three empty apartments on this floor.
One of them has to be unlocked.
Not this one.
Maybe this. The lock looks broken.
I knew it!
I am soooo smart!
Tonight you sleep on the floor. OK? Tomorrow I'll go shopping. I'll bring back a pillow and a blanket. A bed is too big to get out of the store without them noticing.
You can't do this, Annie.

Chapter Fifteen: Stakeout

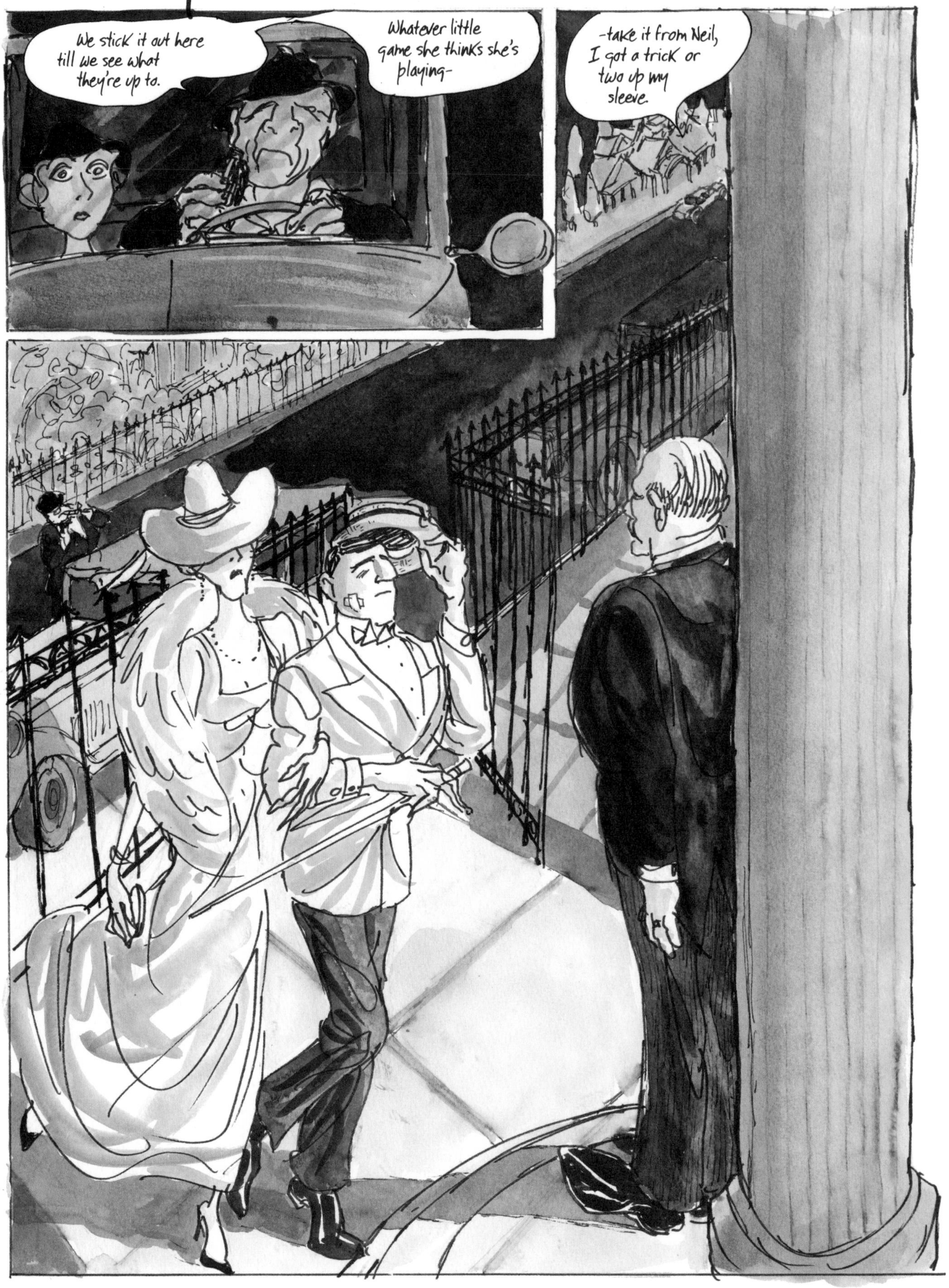
We stick it out here till we see what they're up to.
Whatever little game she thinks she's playing-
-take it from Neil, I got a trick or two up my sleeve.

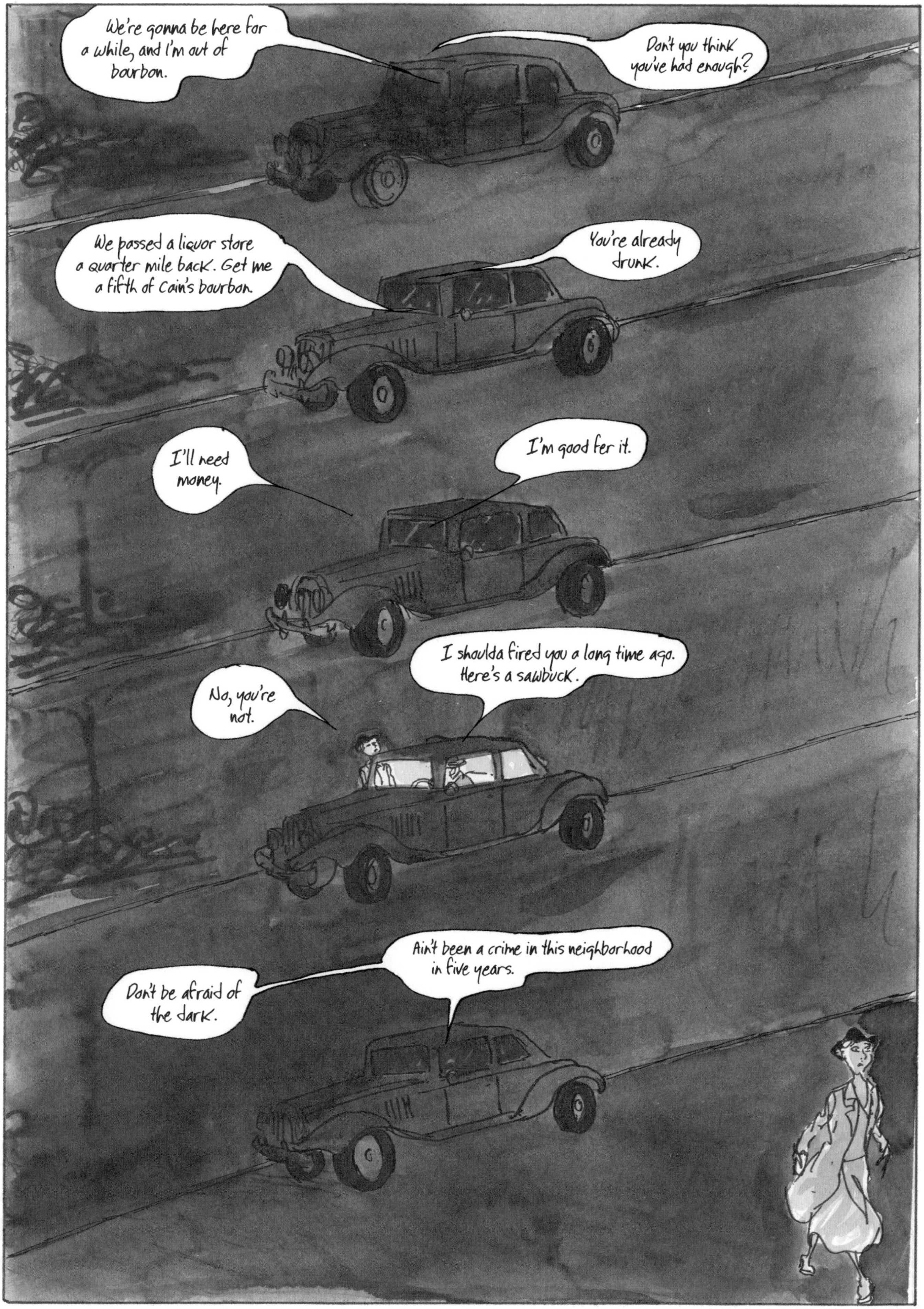
We're gonna be here for a while, and I'm out of bourbon.
Don't you think you've had enough?
We passed a liquor store a quarter mile back. Get me a fifth of Cain's bourbon.
You're already drunk.
I'll need money.
I'm good for it.
No, you're not.
I shoulda fired you a long time ago. Here's a sawbuck.
Don't be afraid of the dark.
Ain't been a crime in this neighborhood in five years.

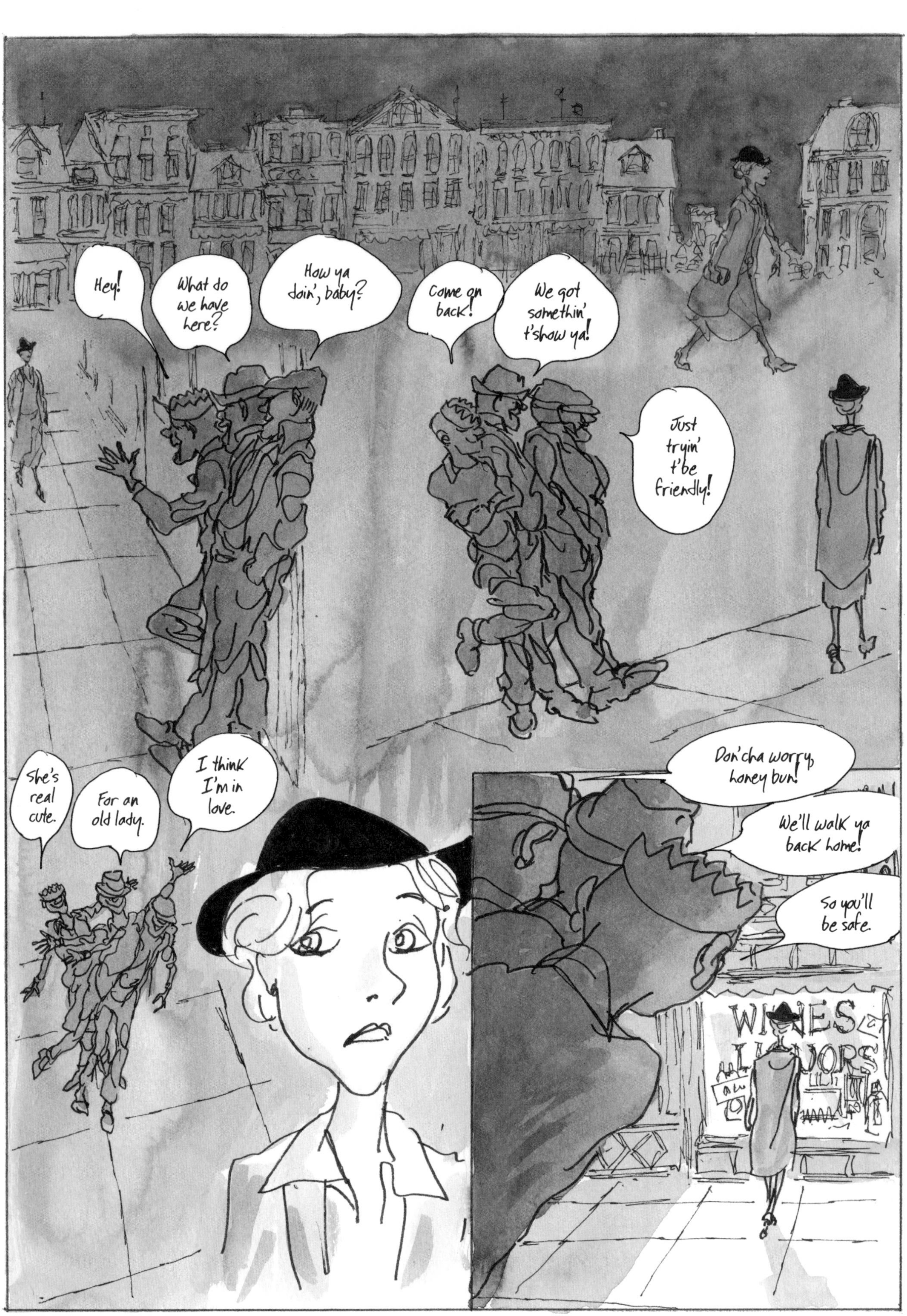
Hey!
What do we have here?
How ya doin', baby?
Come on back!
We got somethin' t'show ya!
Just tryin' t'be friendly!
She's real cute.
For an old lady.
I think I'm in love.
Don'cha worry, honey bun!
We'll walk ya back home!
So you'll be safe.
WINES LIQUORS

Chapter Sixteen: The Elsie Blues

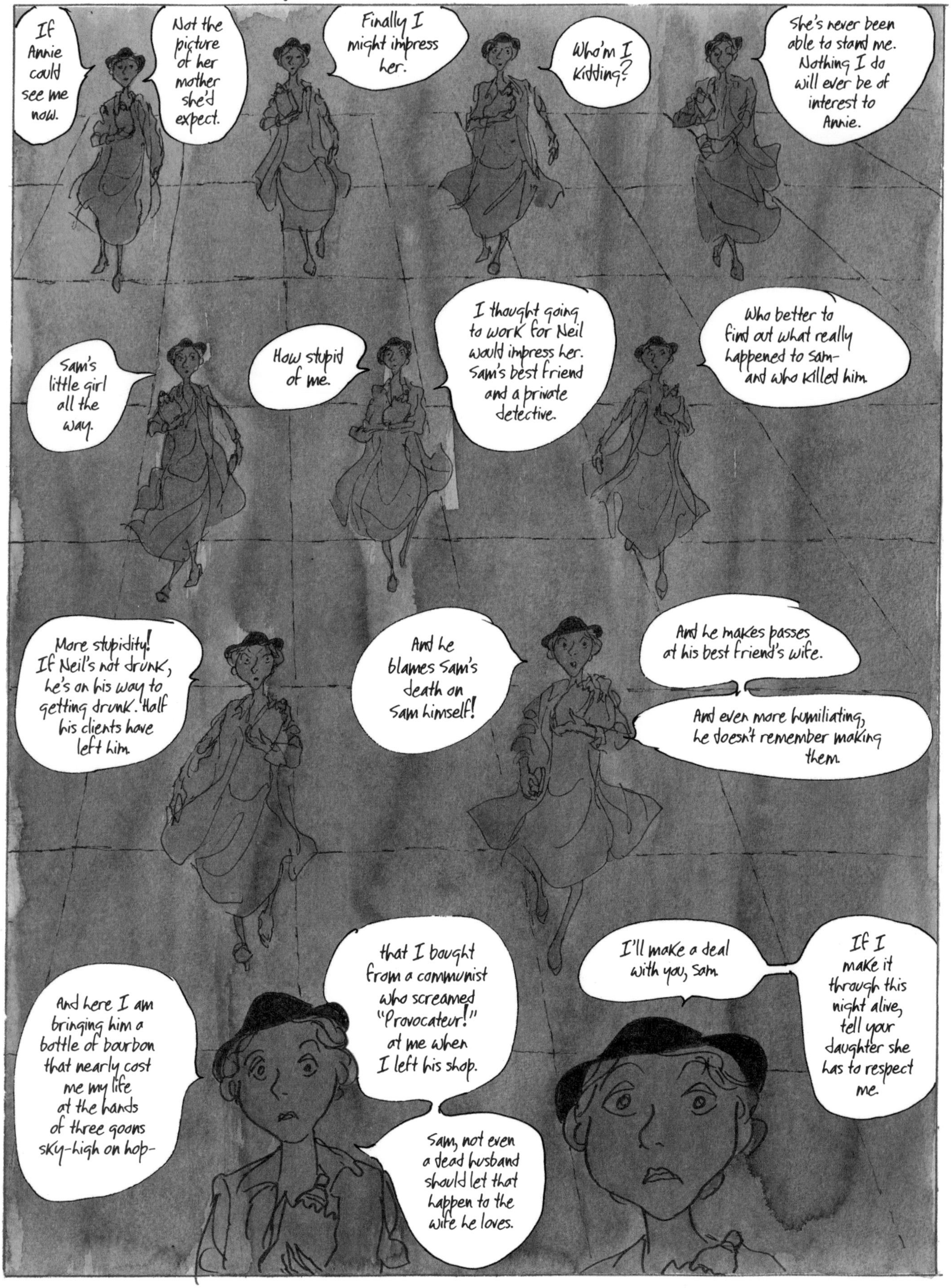

If Annie could see me now.
Not the picture of her mother she'd expect.
Finally I might impress her.
Who'm I kidding?
She's never been able to stand me. Nothing I do will ever be of interest to Annie.
Sam's little girl all the way.
How stupid of me.
I thought going to work for Neil would impress her. Sam's best friend and a private detective.
Who better to find out what really happened to Sam– and who killed him.
More stupidity! If Neil's not drunk, he's on his way to getting drunk. Half his clients have left him.
And he blames Sam's death on Sam himself!
And he makes passes at his best friend's wife.
And even more humiliating, he doesn't remember making them.
And here I am bringing him a bottle of bourbon that nearly cost me my life at the hands of three goons sky-high on hop–
that I bought from a communist who screamed "Provocateur!" at me when I left his shop.
Sam, not even a dead husband should let that happen to the wife he loves.
I'll make a deal with you, Sam.
If I make it through this night alive, tell your daughter she has to respect me.

Chapter Seventeen: Car Chase

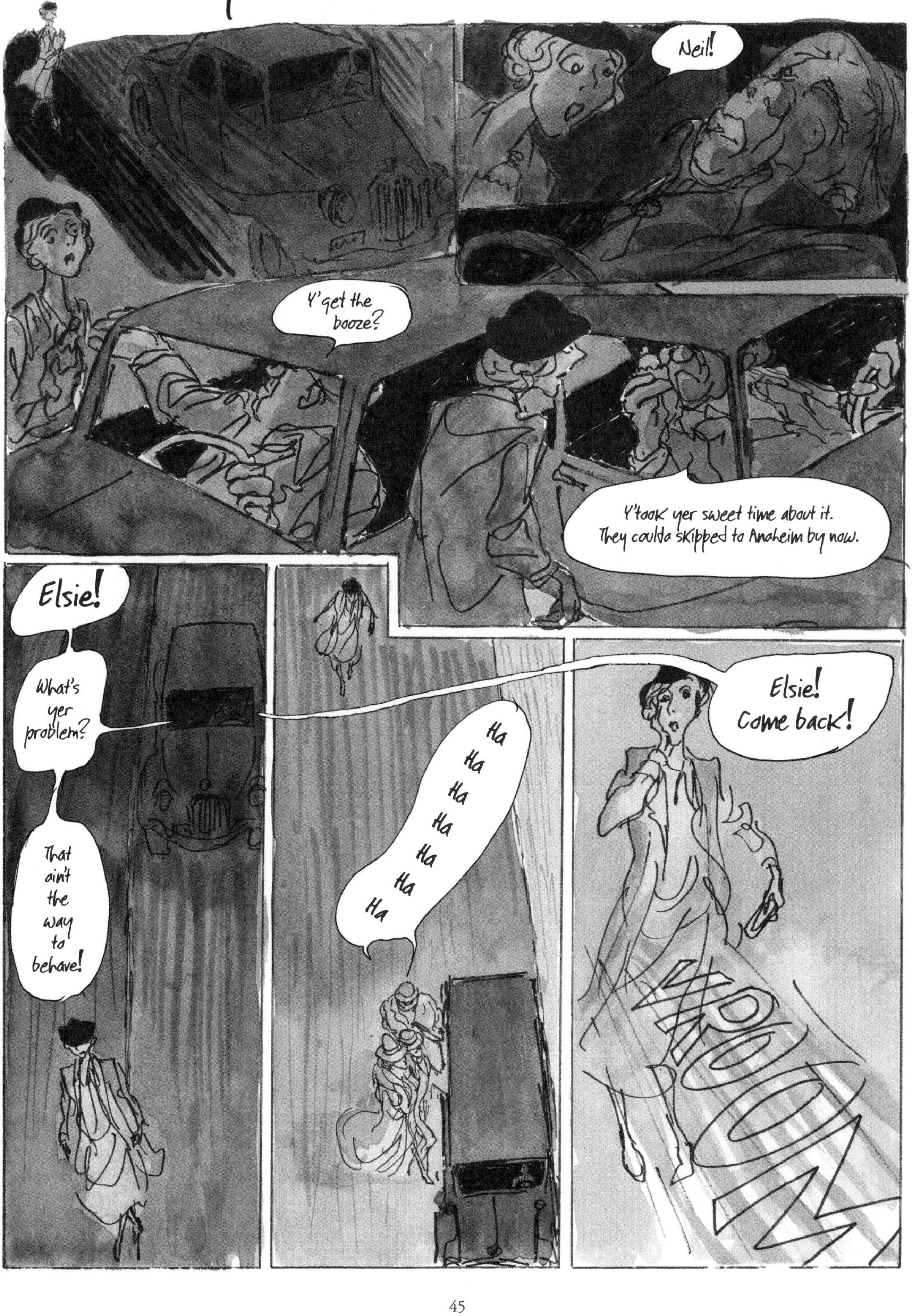
Neil!
Y'get the booze?
Y'took yer sweet time about it. They coulda skipped to Anaheim by now.
Elsie!
What's yer problem?
That ain't the way to behave!
Ha Ha Ha Ha Ha Ha Ha
Elsie! Come back!
VROOOOM

46

47

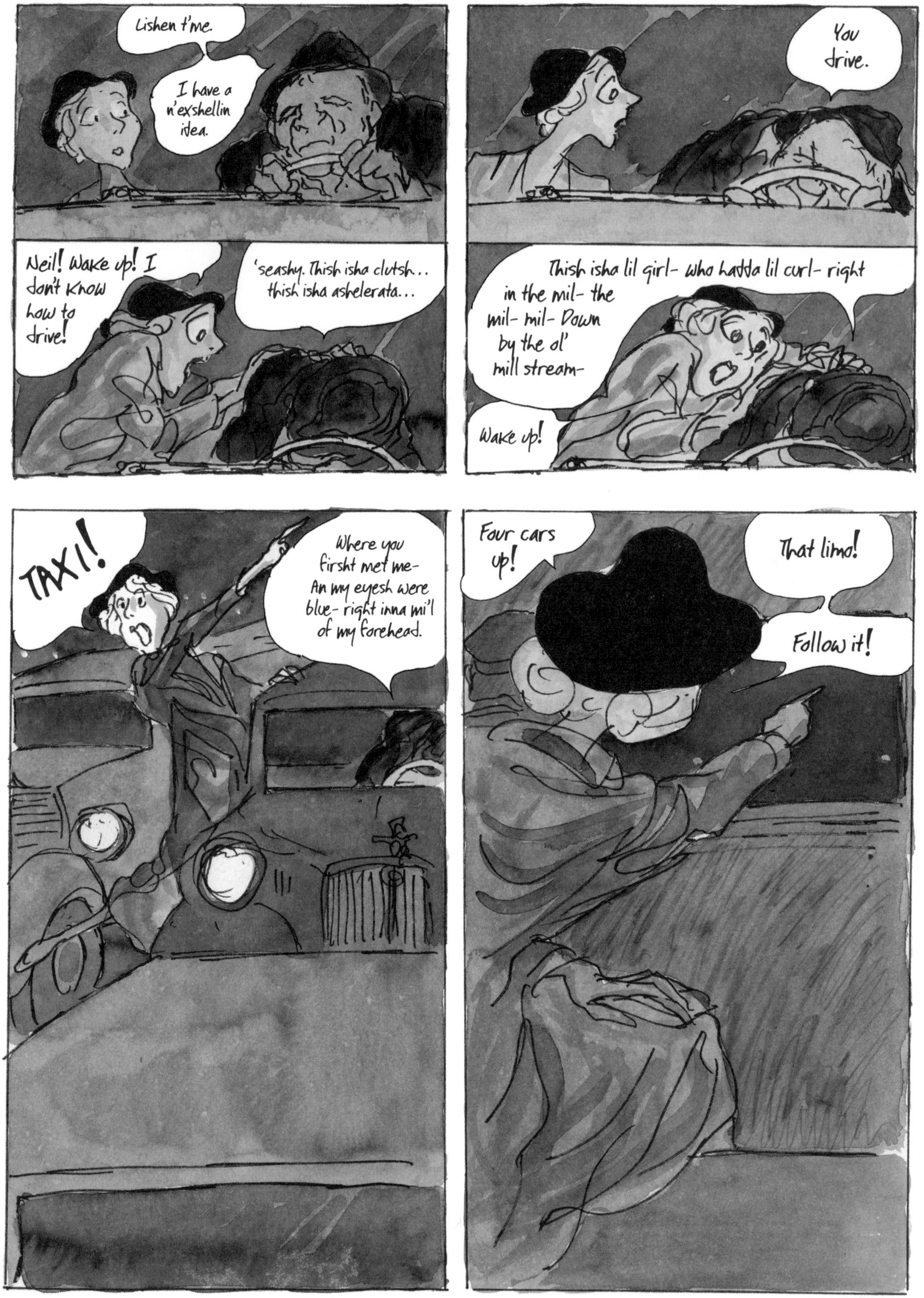
Lishen t'me.
I have a n'exshellin idea.
You drive.
Neil! Wake up! I don't know how to drive!
'seashy. Thish isha clutsh.. thish isha ashelerata...
Thish isha lil girl- who hadda lil curl- right in the mil- the mil- mil- Down by the ol' mill stream-
Wake up!
TAXI!
Where you firsht met me- An my eyesh were blue- right inna mi'l of my forehead.
Four cars up!
That limo!
Follow it!

Follow that limo? I thought I heard 'em all, but on my mother's grave—

Now, follow that blonde— that one I got last month, right here on Main street—

But it was Carole Lombard. You couldn't mistake her! Carole Lombard in Bay City! Window shopping! As if she needs to shop in Bay City.

"No!" I say t'myself, "It can't be her!" Small, tiny, but beautiful. Don't get me wrong, lady, you're nice looking too.

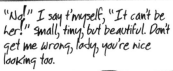

But Carole Lombard? I'm as close to her as I am to you. Except, I'm here in the front seat, and she's on Main, corner of Peach-tree.

Stop it! Stop it! Stop it!

Don't you recognize me, you stupid fool? I'm Jean Harlow!

Now, shut up and follow that limo!

No one's gonna believe me.

First, Carole Lombard and then Jean Harlow, what are the odds? Although in person, you don't look that much like her, but neither did Carole Lombard.

Chapter Eighteen: 7 AM

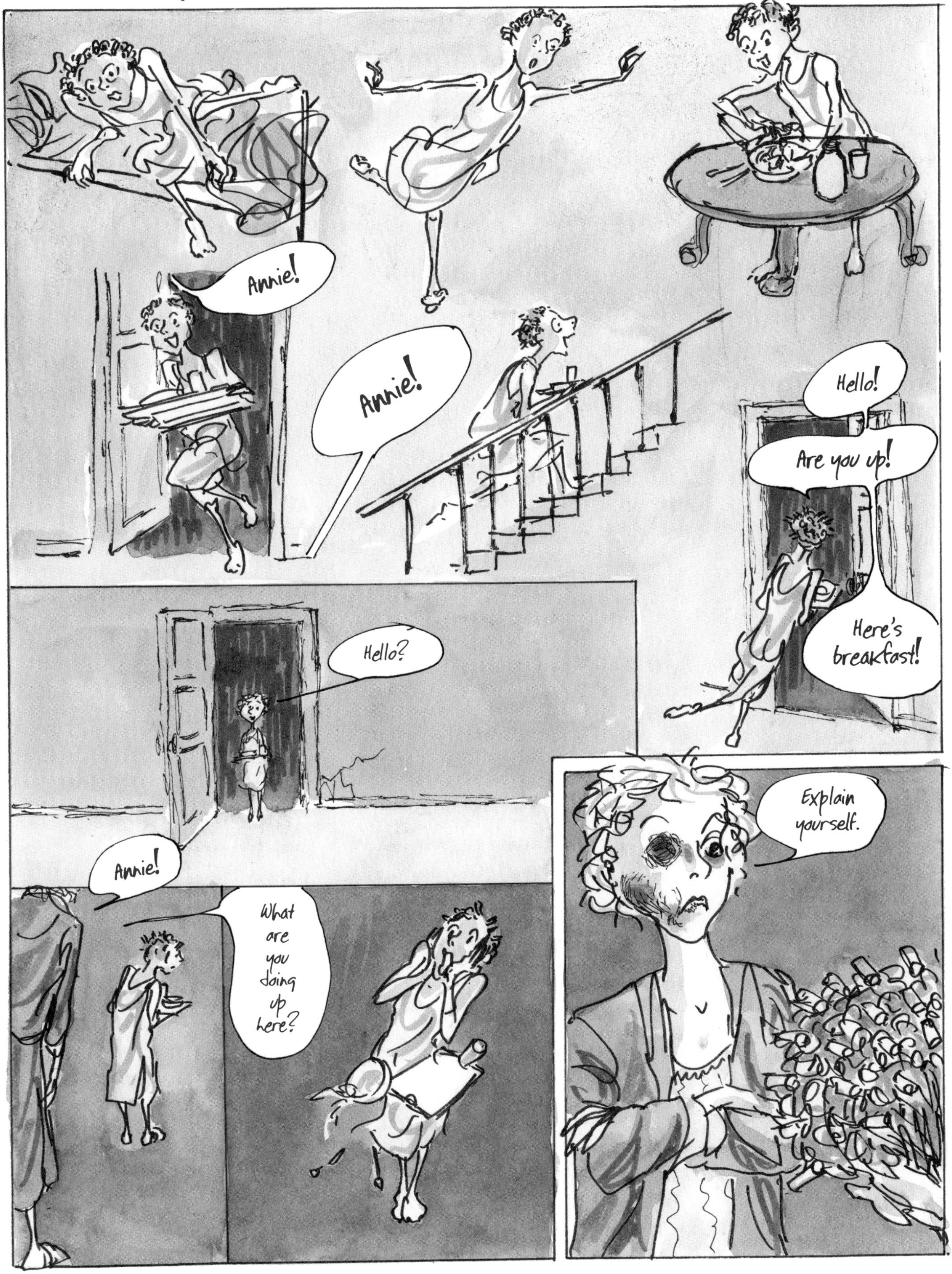
Annie!
Annie!
Hello!
Are you up!
Here's breakfast!
Hello?
Annie!
What are you doing up here?
Explain yourself.

Chapter Nineteen: Casting Call

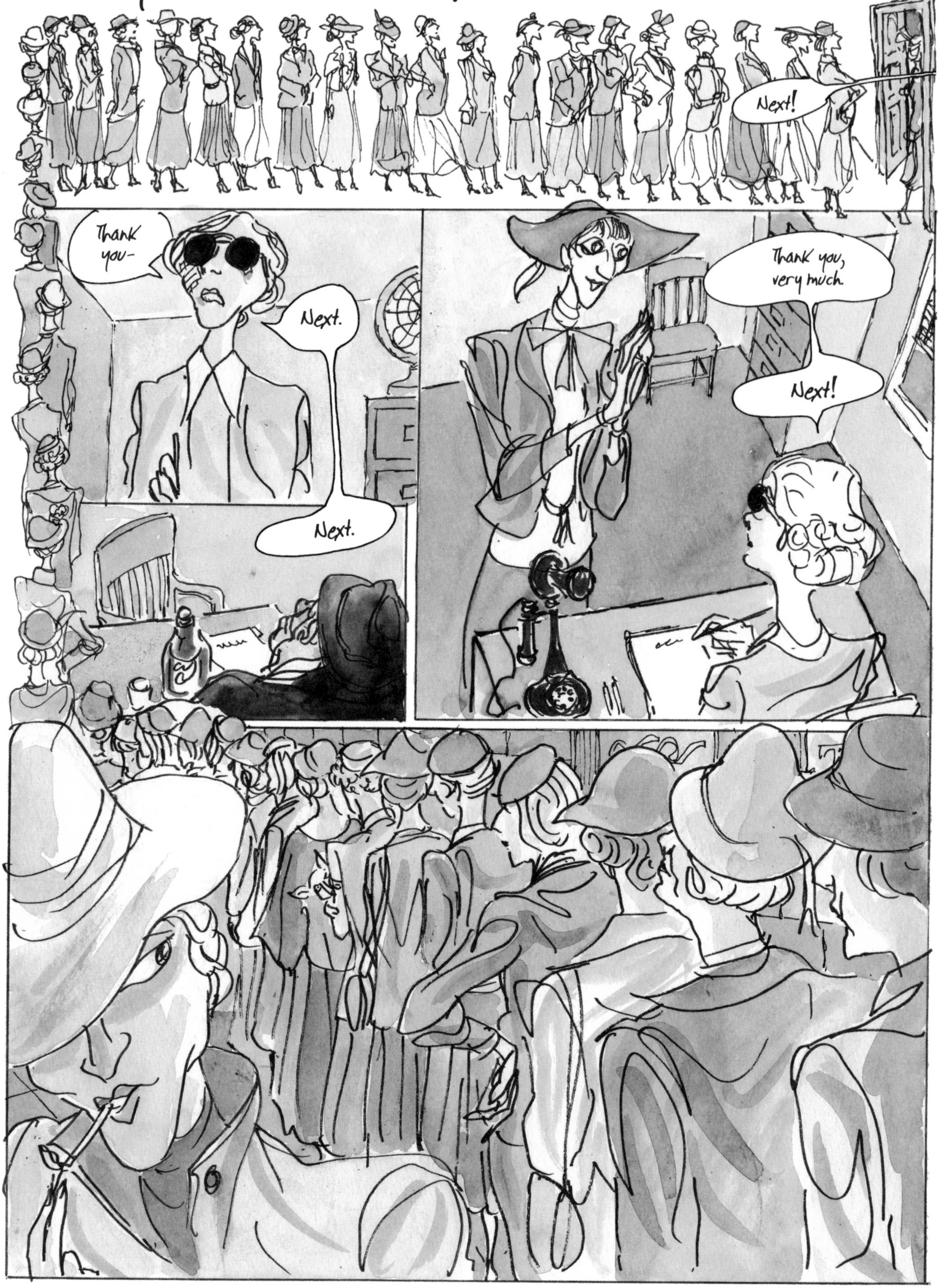

Chapter Twenty: The Interview

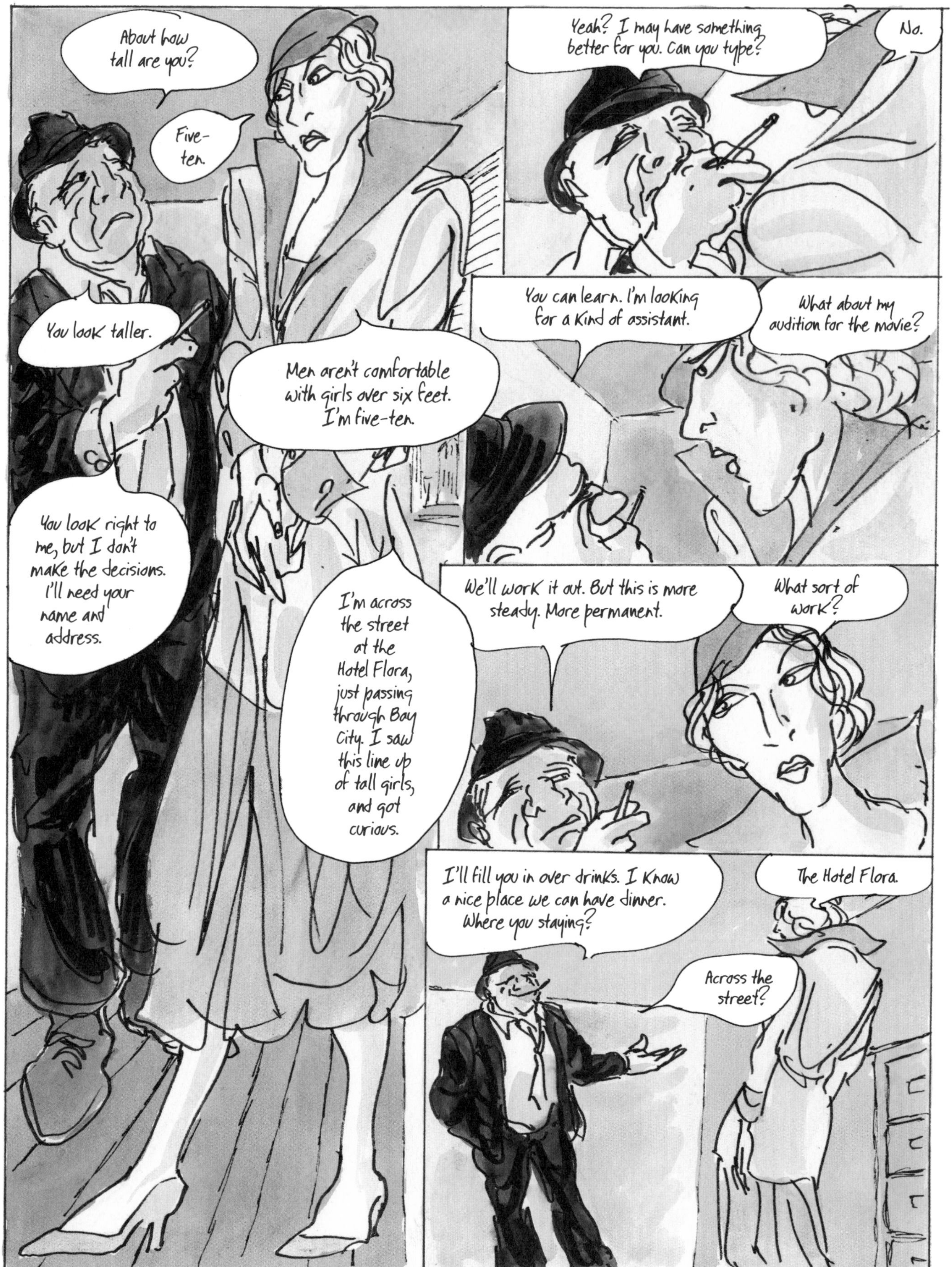

About how tall are you?
Five-ten.
You look taller.
Men aren't comfortable with girls over six feet. I'm five-ten.
You look right to me, but I don't make the decisions. I'll need your name and address.
I'm across the street at the Hotel Flora, just passing through Bay City. I saw this line up of tall girls, and got curious.
Yeah? I may have something better for you. Can you type?
No.
You can learn. I'm looking for a kind of assistant.
What about my audition for the movie?
We'll work it out. But this is more steady. More permanent.
What sort of work?
I'll fill you in over drinks. I know a nice place we can have dinner. Where you staying?
The Hotel Flora.
Across the street?

55

Chapter Twenty-One: There Was a Little Girl

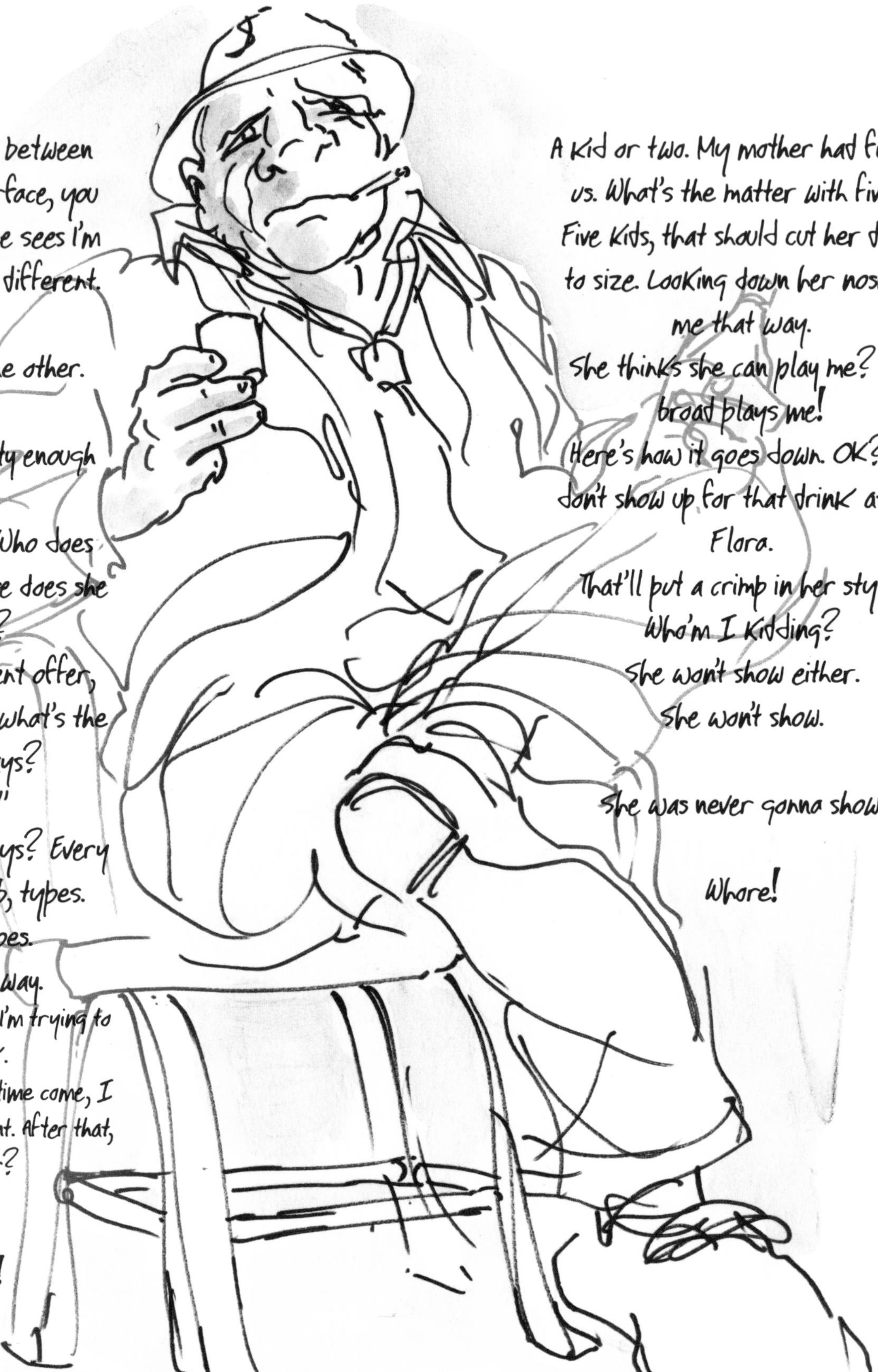

Something was goin'on between us. I felt it. On the surface, you could miss it . . . that she sees I'm not like the others. I'm different. Dangerous.

She makes fools of the other.

But not me.

She's big. But I'm plenty enough man for her.

Looking down on me. Who does she think she is? Where does she get the nerve?

I come up with a decent offer, cards on the table. And what's the first thing she says?

"I can't type."

Who can't type these days? Every broad, she wants a job, types.

Trust me, she types.

Mocking me that way.

She was mocking me. When I'm trying to give her a break.

I start her out typing- The time come, I promote her- To my assistant. After that, what's to stop her?

Nothing!

We get married!

A kid or two. My mother had five of us. What's the matter with five? Five kids, that should cut her down to size. Looking down her nose at me that way.

She thinks she can play me? No broad plays me!

Here's how it goes down. OK? I don't show up for that drink at the Flora.

That'll put a crimp in her style.

Who'm I kidding?

She won't show either.

She won't show.

She was never gonna show.

Whore!

Chapter Twenty-Two: Right in the Middle Of Her Forehead

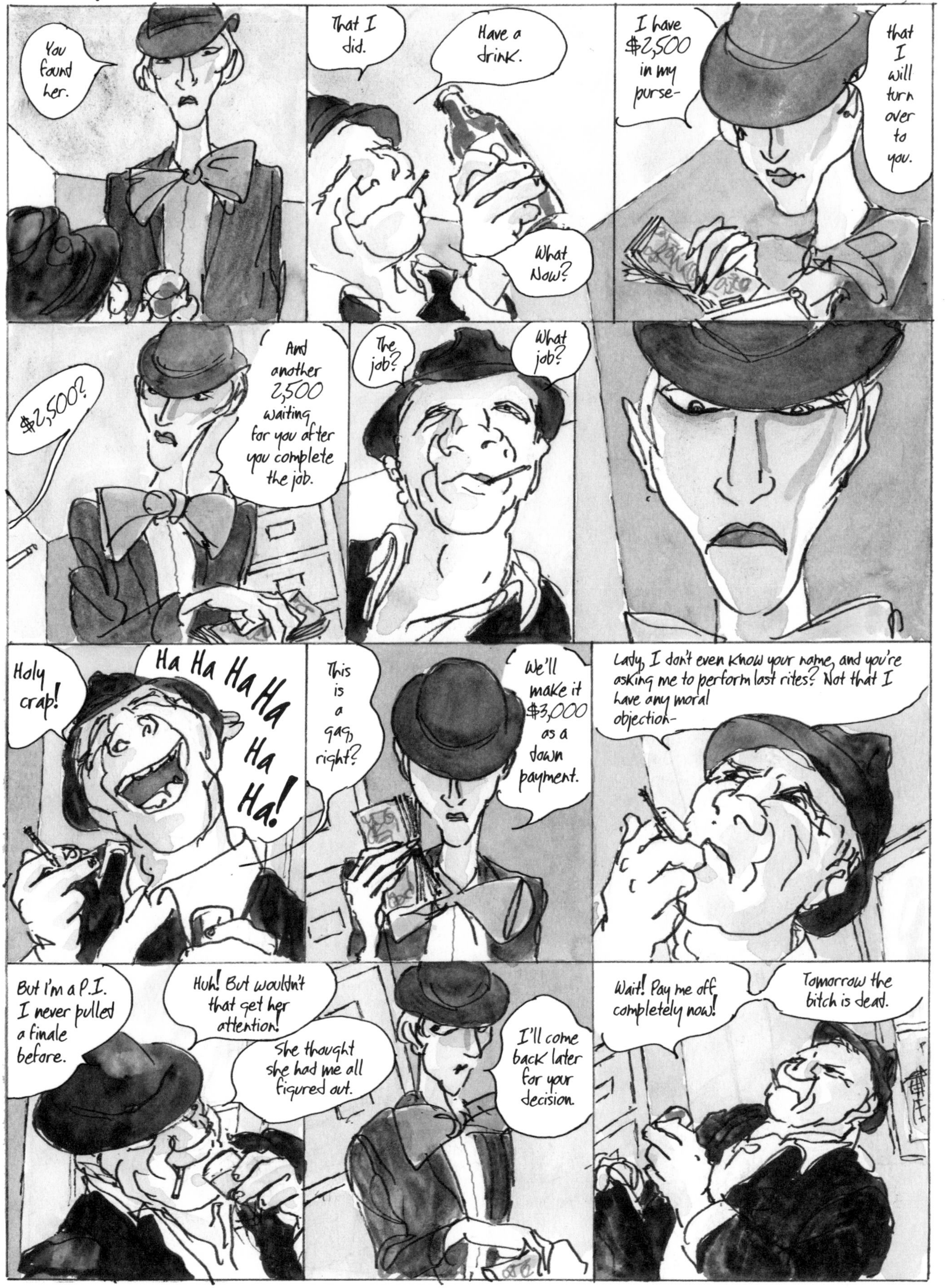

You found her.
That I did.
Have a drink.
What Now?
I have $2,500 in my purse-
that I will turn over to you.
$2,500?
And another 2,500 waiting for you after you complete the job.
The job?
What job?
Holy crap!
Ha Ha Ha Ha Ha Ha!
This is a gag, right?
We'll make it $3,000 as a down payment.
Lady, I don't even know your name, and you're asking me to perform last rites? Not that I have any moral objection-
But I'm a P.I. I never pulled a finale before.
Huh! But wouldn't that get her attention!
She thought she had me all figured out.
I'll come back later for your decision.
Wait! Pay me off completely now!
Tomorrow the bitch is dead.

Chapter Twenty-Three: A Night at the Flora

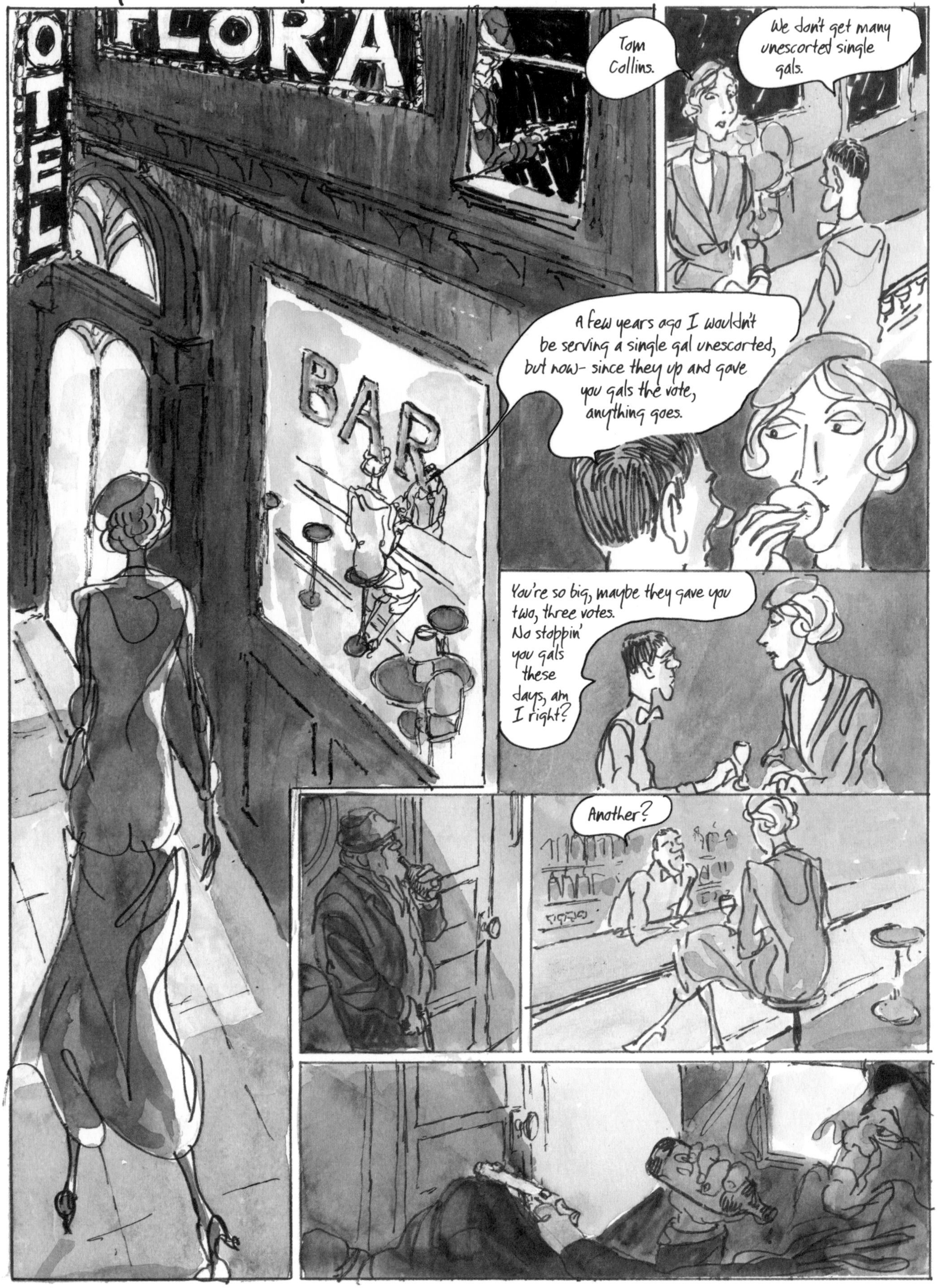
HOTEL
FLORA
Tom Collins.
We don't get many unescorted single gals.
BAR
A few years ago I wouldn't be serving a single gal unescorted, but now- since they up and gave you gals the vote, anything goes.
You're so big, maybe they gave you two, three votes. No stoppin' you gals these days, am I right?
Another?

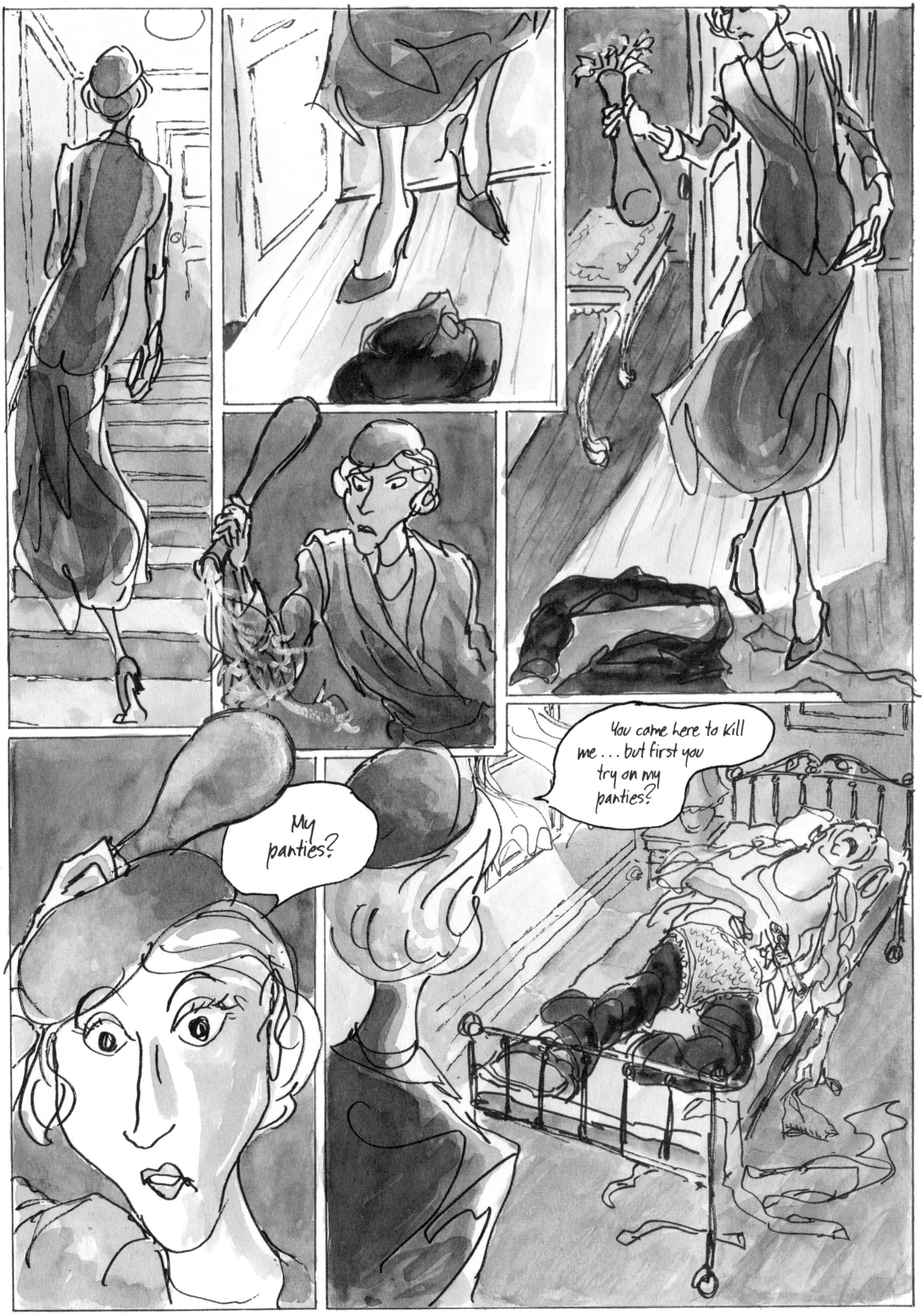
My panties?
You came here to kill me . . . but first you try on my panties?

Mother.

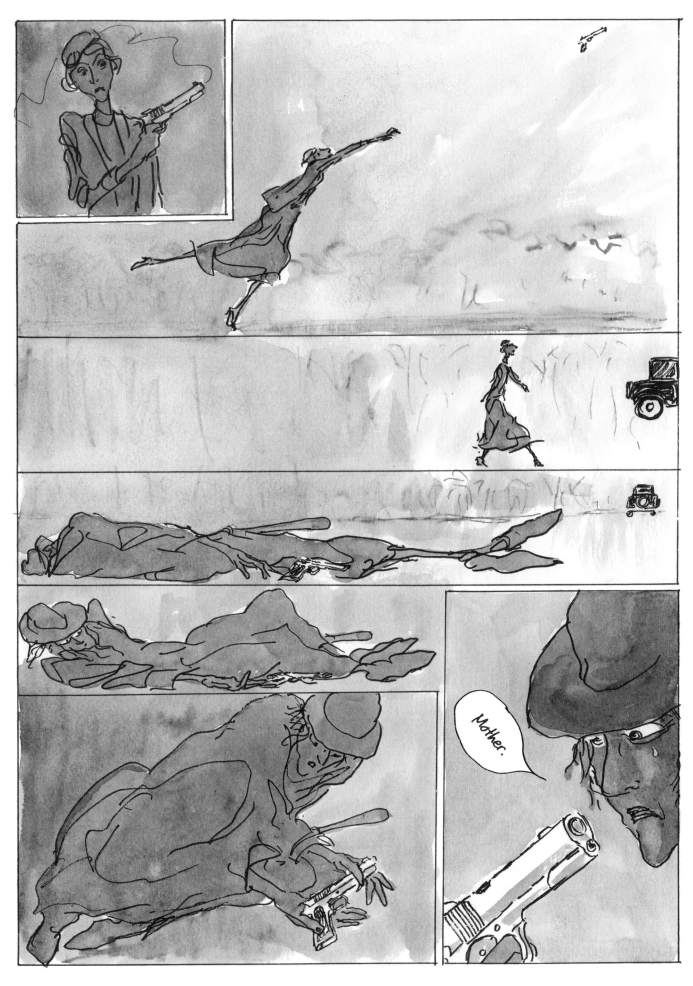

62

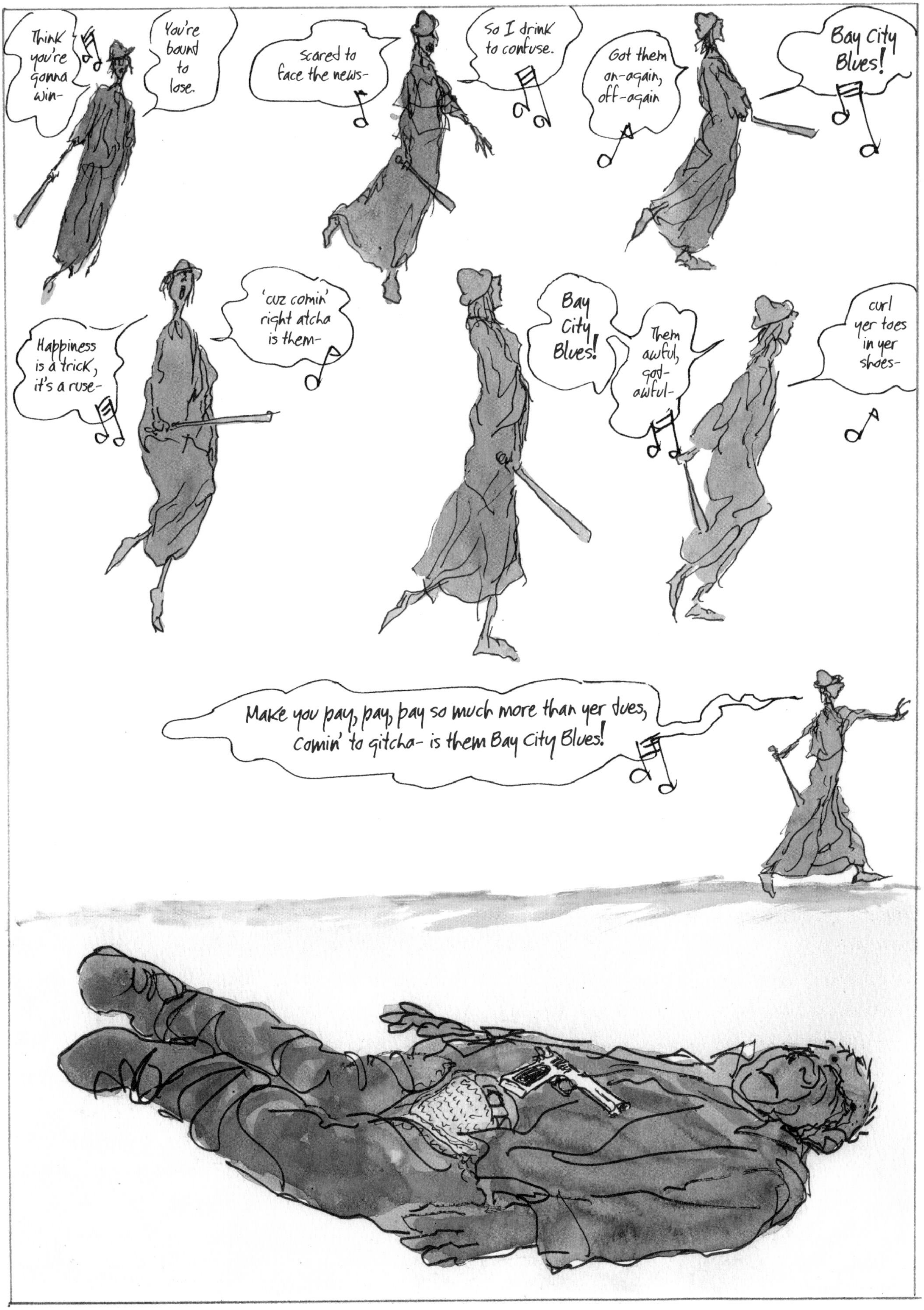
Think you're gonna win-
You're bound to lose.
Scared to face the news-
So I drink to confuse.
Got them on-again, off-again
Bay City Blues!
Happiness is a trick, it's a ruse-
'cuz comin' right atcha is them-
Bay City Blues!
Them awful, god-awful-
curl yer toes in yer shoes-
Make you pay, pay, pay so much more than yer dues, comin' to gitcha- is them Bay City Blues!

Part Two:

Hooray For Hollywood
1943

Chapter One: "Shut Up, Artie!"

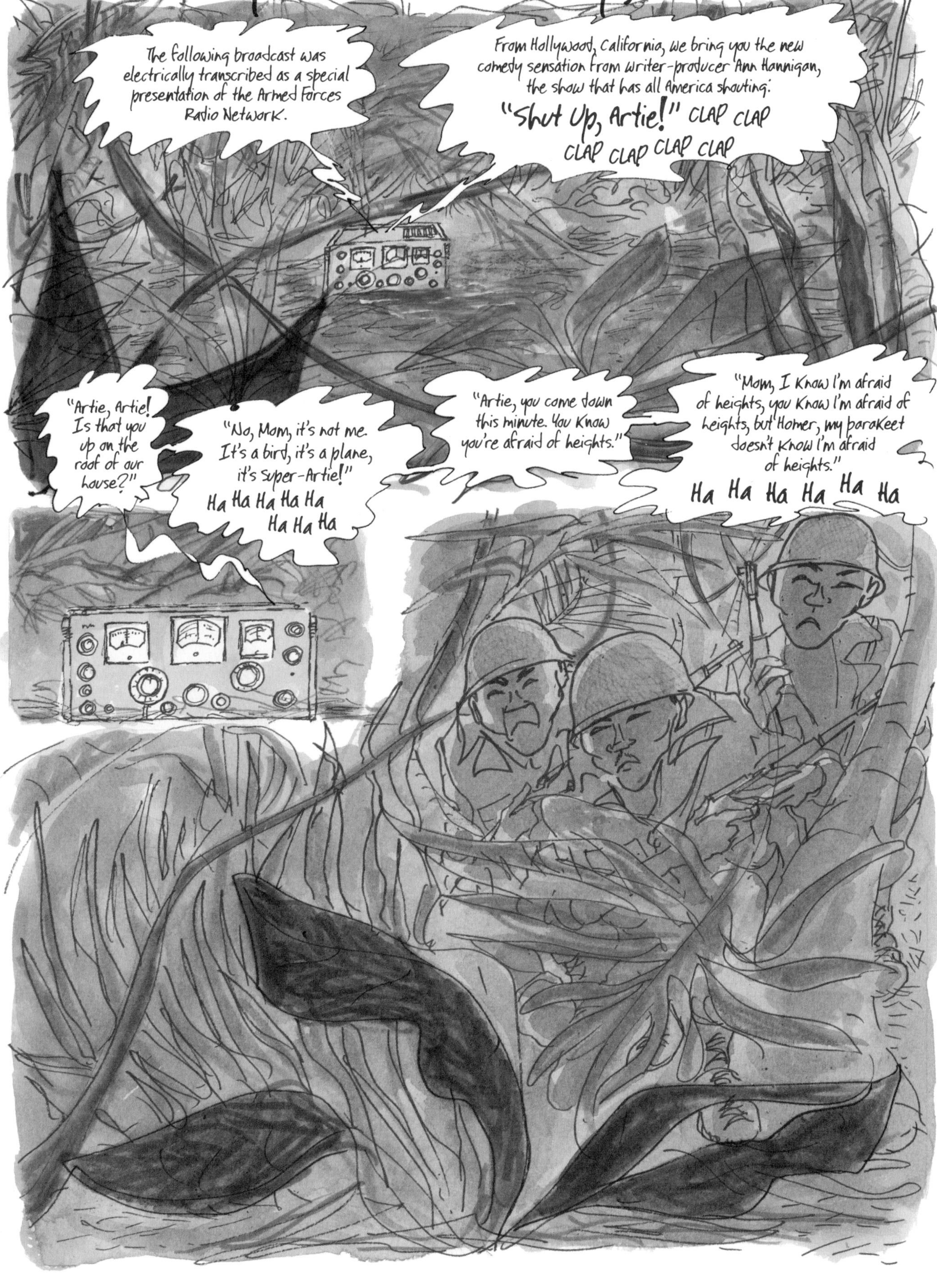
The following broadcast was electrically transcribed as a special presentation of the Armed Forces Radio Network.
From Hollywood, California, we bring you the new comedy sensation from writer-producer Ann Hannigan, the show that has all America shouting:
"Shut Up, Artie!" CLAP CLAP CLAP CLAP CLAP CLAP
"Artie, Artie! Is that you up on the roof of our house?"
"No, Mom, it's not me. It's a bird, it's a plane, it's super-Artie!" Ha Ha Ha Ha Ha Ha Ha Ha Ha
"Artie, you come down this minute. You know you're afraid of heights."
"Mom, I know I'm afraid of heights, you know I'm afraid of heights, but Homer, my parakeet doesn't know I'm afraid of heights."
Ha Ha Ha Ha Ha Ha

"And Homer got out of his cage, Mom — and flew up here on the roof — and I crawled up here to get him down — but Mom, Mom! Who's gonna get **me** down?"

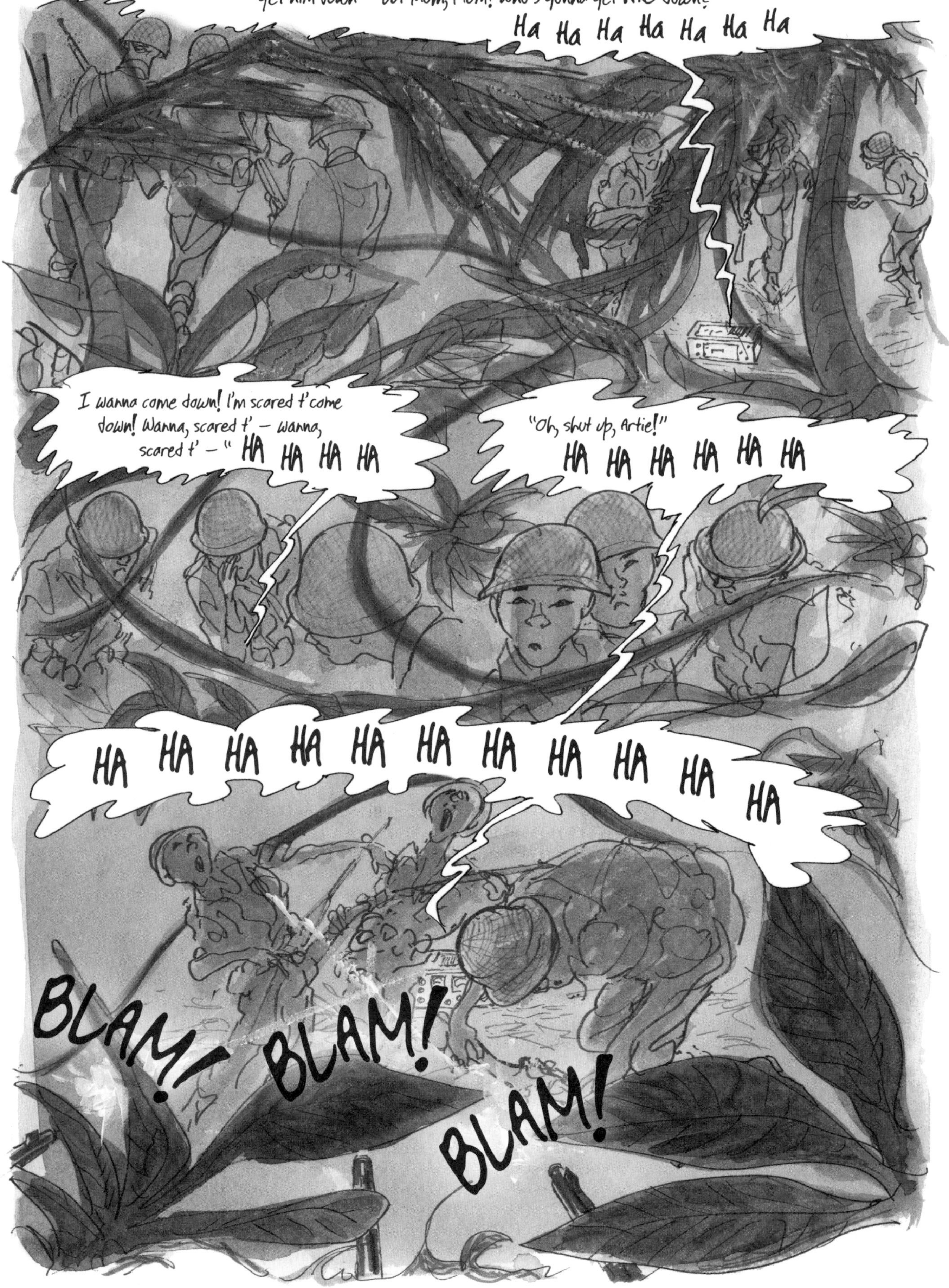

Chapter Two: Little Sammy Hannigan

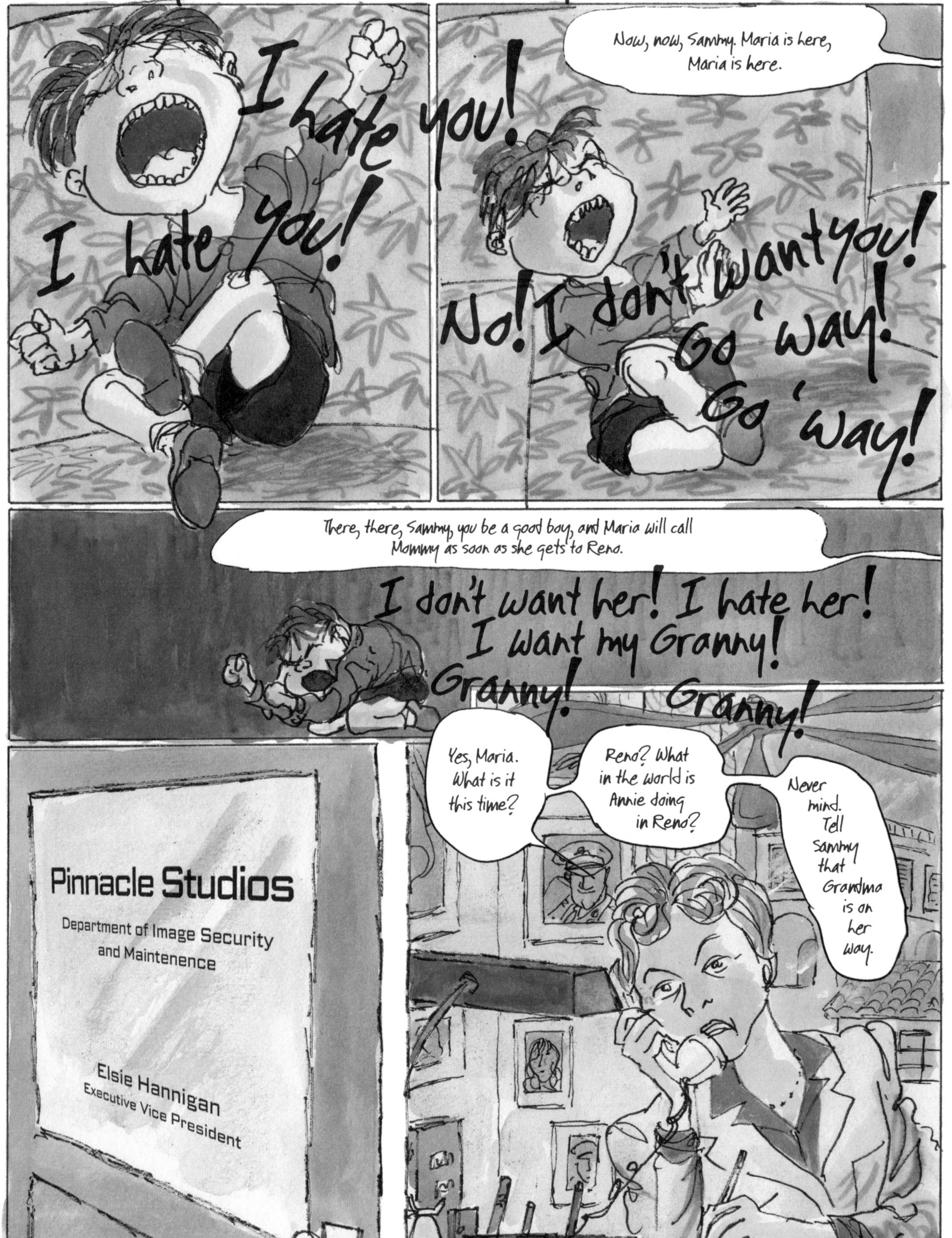

I hate you! I hate you!
Now, now, Sammy. Maria is here, Maria is here.
No! I don't want you! Go 'way! Go 'way!
There, there, Sammy, you be a good boy, and Maria will call Mommy as soon as she gets to Reno.
I don't want her! I hate her! I want my Granny! Granny! Granny!
Pinnacle Studios
Department of Image Security and Maintenence
Elsie Hannigan
Executive Vice President
Yes, Maria. What is it this time?
Reno? What in the world is Annie doing in Reno?
Never mind. Tell Sammy that Grandma is on her way.

Chapter Three: Lady Veil

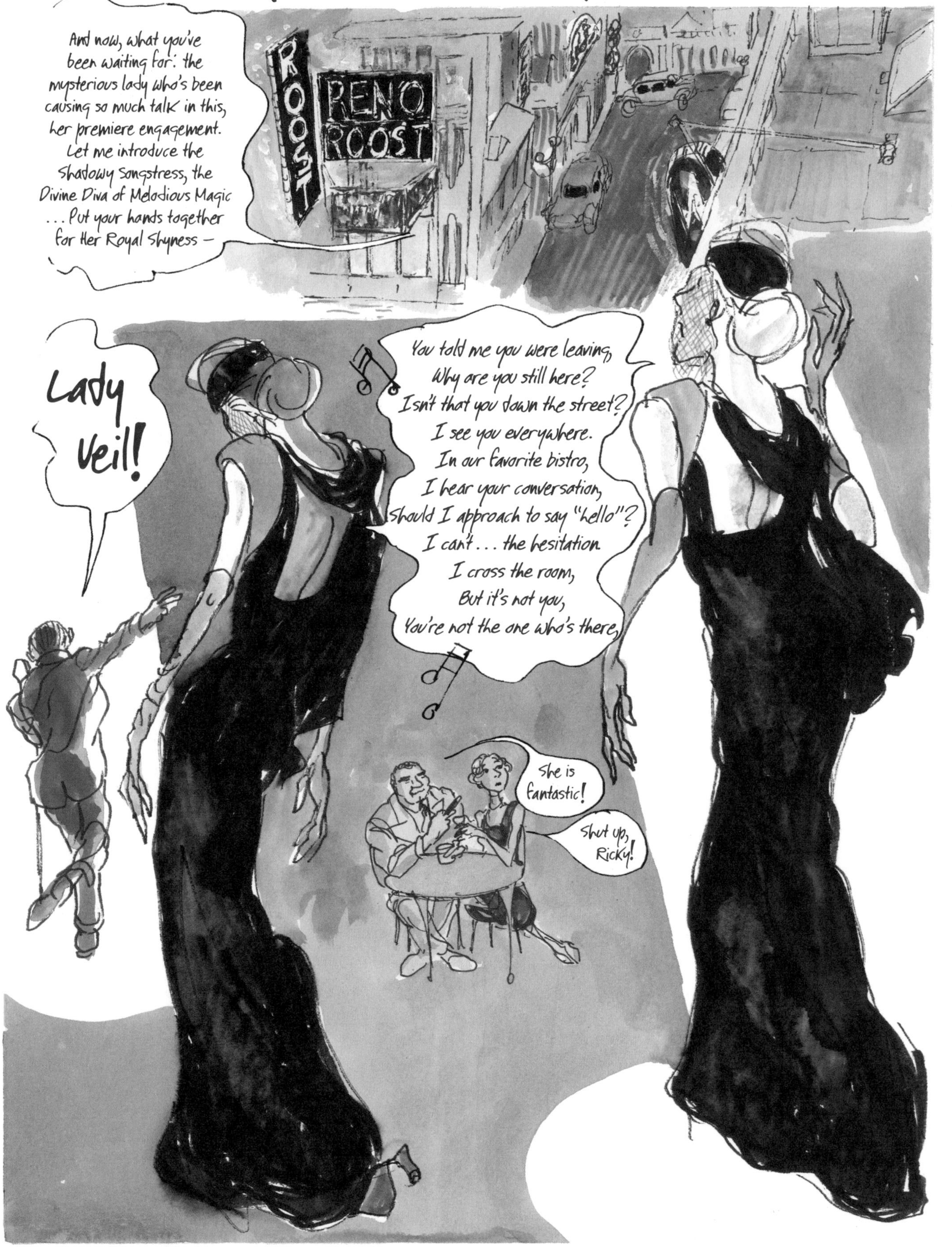

And now, what you've been waiting for: the mysterious lady who's been causing so much talk in this, her premiere engagement. Let me introduce the Shadowy Songstress, the Divine Diva of Melodious Magic . . . Put your hands together for Her Royal Shyness —
ROOST
RENO ROOST
Lady Veil!
You told me you were leaving, Why are you still here? Isn't that you down the street? I see you everywhere. In our favorite bistro, I hear your conversation, Should I approach to say "hello"? I can't . . . the hesitation. I cross the room, But it's not you, You're not the one who's there,
She is fantastic!
Shut up, Ricky!

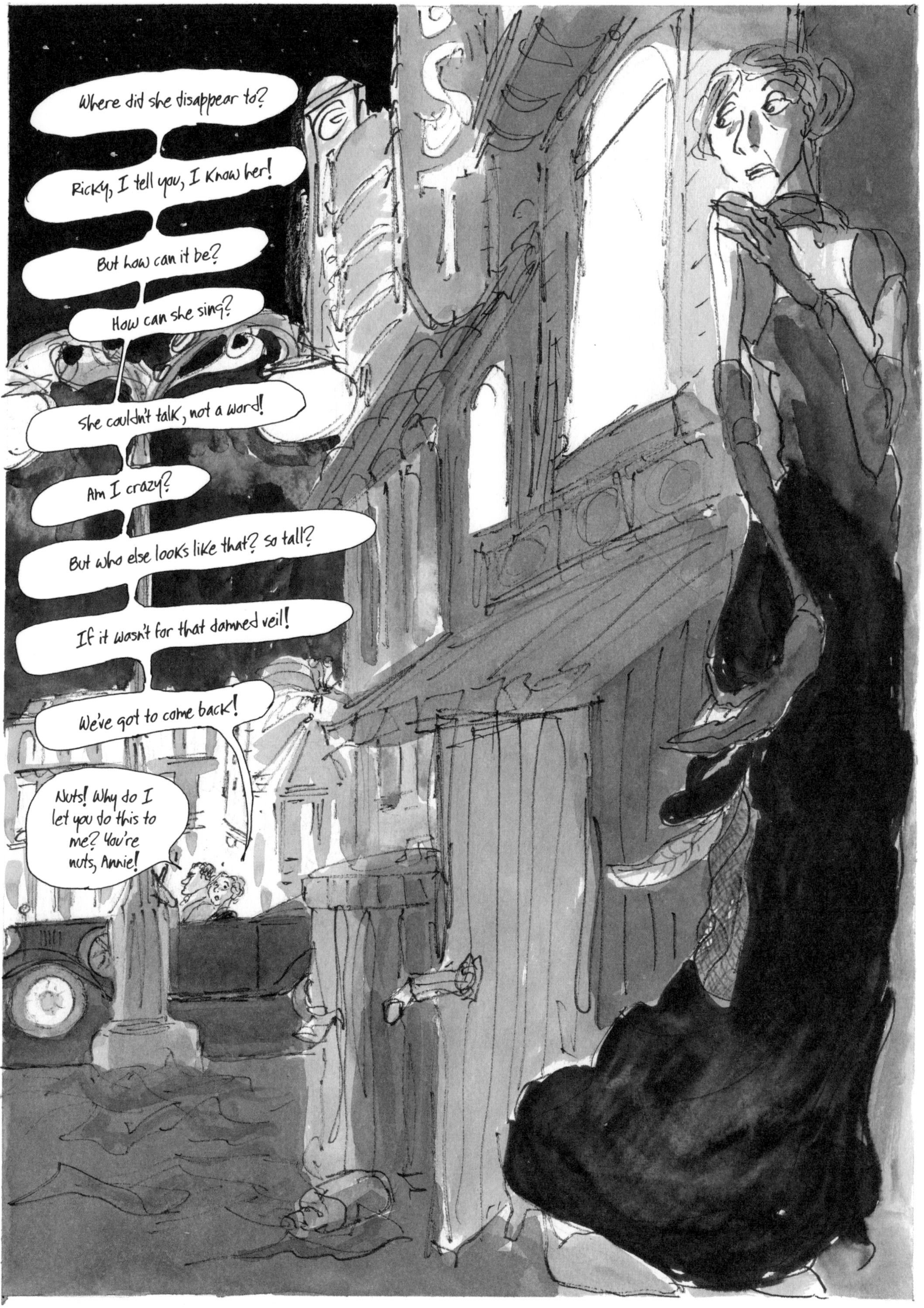
Where did she disappear to?
Ricky, I tell you, I know her!
But how can it be?
How can she sing?
She couldn't talk, not a word!
Am I crazy?
But who else looks like that? so tall?
If it wasn't for that damned veil!
We've got to come back!
Nuts! Why do I let you do this to me? You're nuts, Annie!

Chapter Four: Little Orphan Sammy

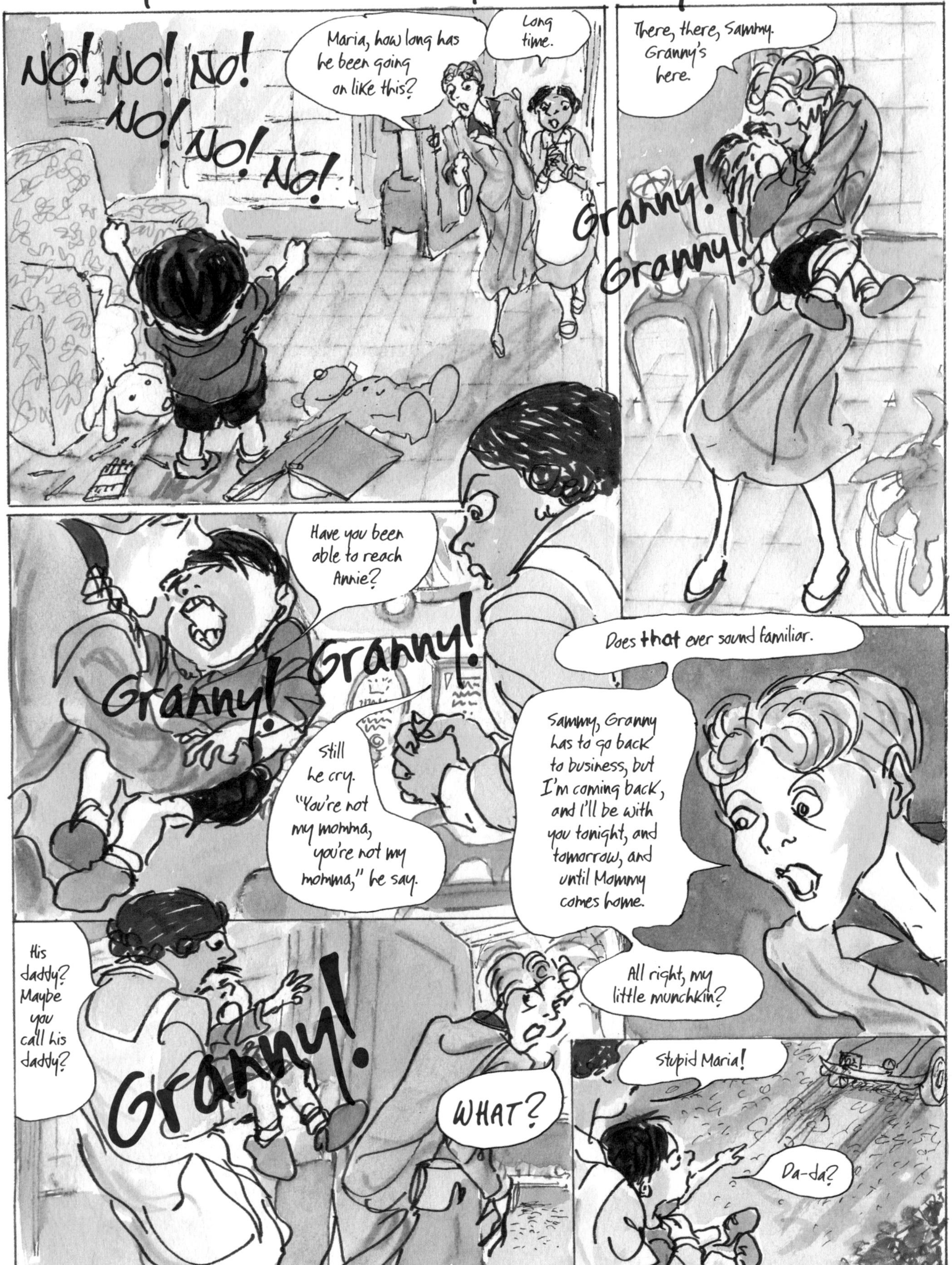
NO! NO! NO! NO! NO! NO!
Maria, how long has he been going on like this?
Long time.
There, there, Sammy. Granny's here.
Granny! Granny!
Have you been able to reach Annie?
Granny! Granny!
Still he cry. "You're not my momma, you're not my momma," he say.
Does that ever sound familiar.
Sammy, Granny has to go back to business, but I'm coming back, and I'll be with you tonight, and tomorrow, and until Mommy comes home.
His daddy? Maybe you call his daddy?
Granny!
WHAT?
All right, my little munchkin?
Stupid Maria!
Da-da?

Chapter Five: Eddie Longo, Take 1

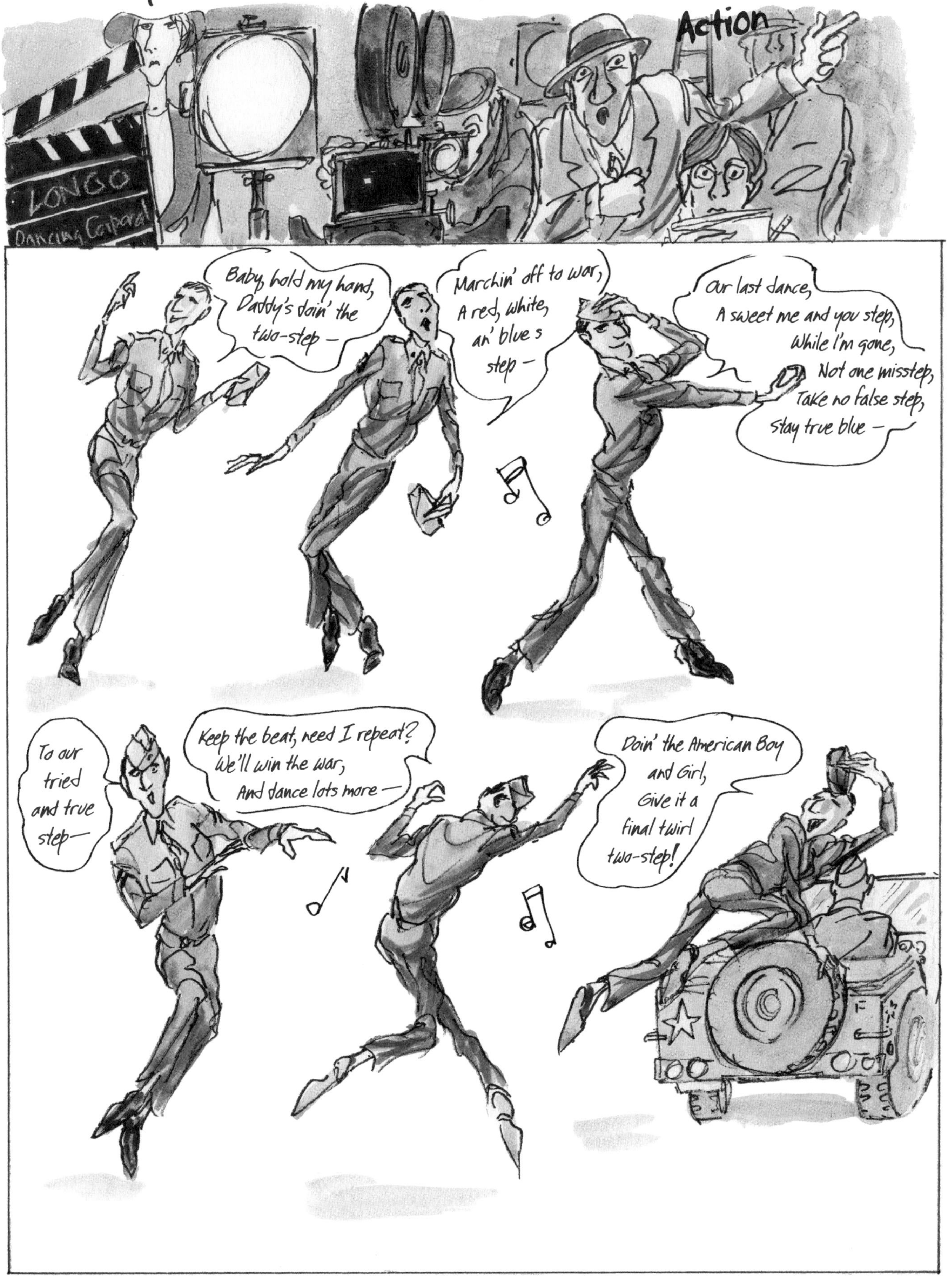
Action
LONGO
Dancing Corporal
Baby, hold my hand, Daddy's doin' the two-step —
Marchin' off to war, A red, white, an' blue s step —
Our last dance, A sweet me and you step, While I'm gone, Not one misstep, Take no false step, Stay true blue —
To our tried and true step—
Keep the beat, need I repeat? We'll win the war, And dance lots more —
Doin' the American Boy and Girl, Give it a final twirl two-step!

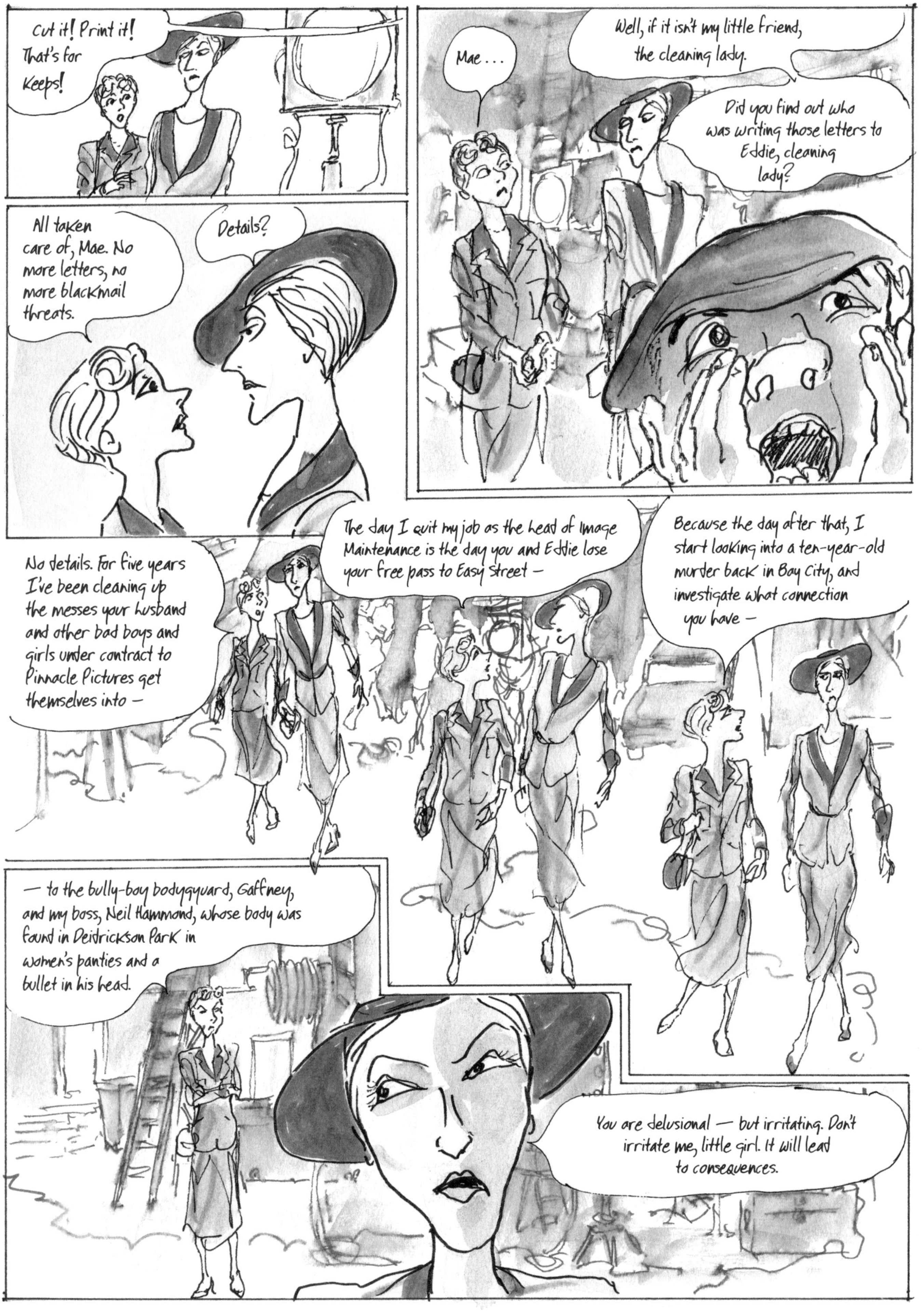
Cut it! Print it! That's for Keeps!
Mae...
Well, if it isn't my little friend, the cleaning lady.
Did you find out who was writing those letters to Eddie, cleaning lady?
All taken care of, Mae. No more letters, no more blackmail threats.
Details?
No details. For five years I've been cleaning up the messes your husband and other bad boys and girls under contract to Pinnacle Pictures get themselves into —
The day I quit my job as the head of Image Maintenance is the day you and Eddie lose your free pass to Easy Street —
Because the day after that, I start looking into a ten-year-old murder back in Bay City, and investigate what connection you have —
— to the bully-boy bodyguard, Gaffney, and my boss, Neil Hammond, whose body was found in Deidrickson Park in women's panties and a bullet in his head.
You are delusional — but irritating. Don't irritate me, little girl. It will lead to consequences.

Chapter Six: Eddie Longo, Take 2

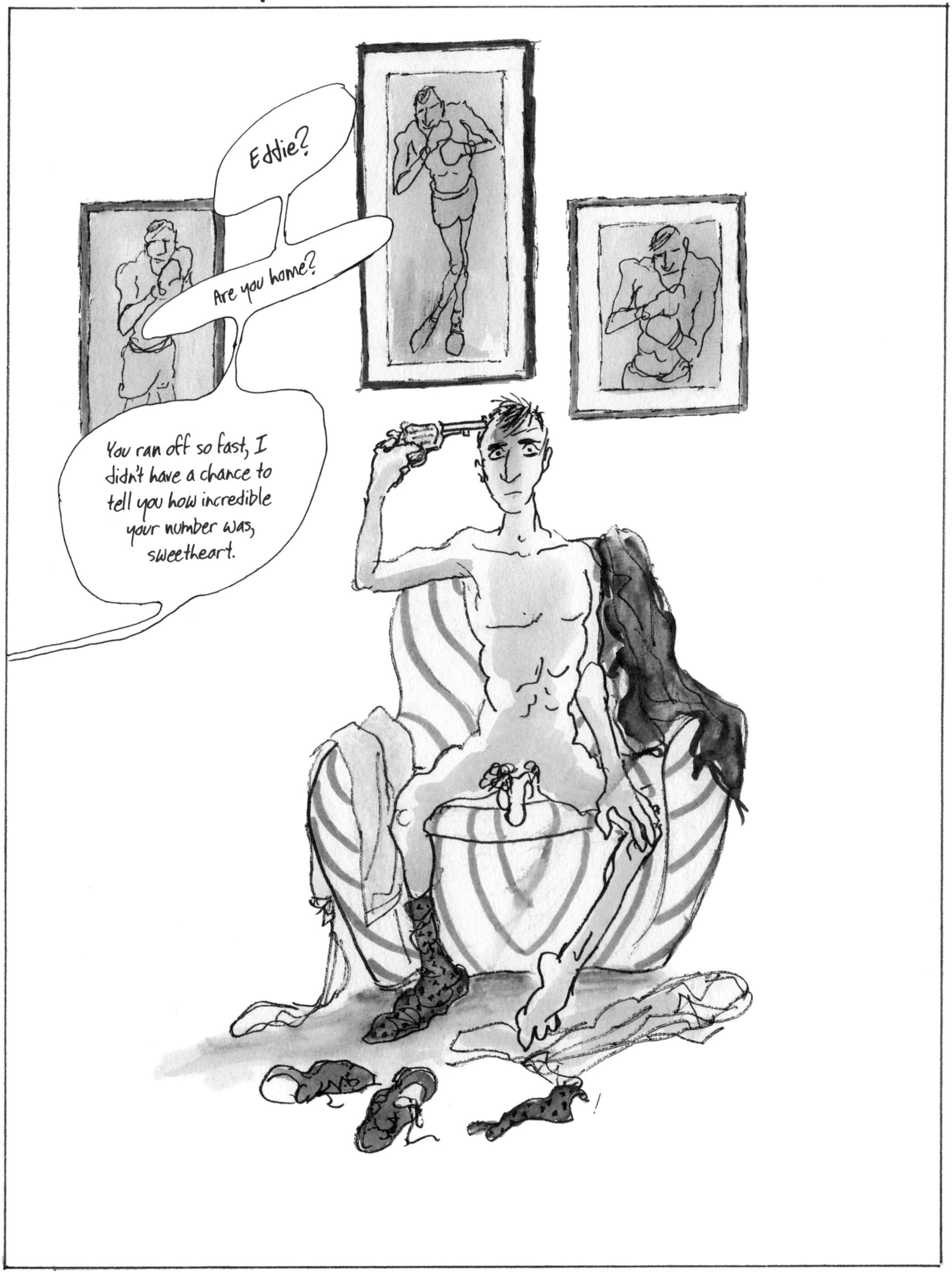
Eddie?
Are you home?
You ran off so fast, I didn't have a chance to tell you how incredible your number was, sweetheart.

79

Chapter Seven: Hollywood Canteen

Did you see him in "Whispering Nights"?

I saw Hugh Patton go in.

He's gorgeous!

Barbara Stanwyck just walked in!

Am I crazy or was that Betty Hutton?

Relax, Miss Hannigan. I'm not as bad as the stories you've heard.

I'm hired to kill those stories, Mr. Patton. And the funny thing I found in checking them out, is that not only were they false, but most of them came from YOU.

I could get you fired for that lie, even if it IS true.

My job is to protect you, not expose you. What I don't understand is why you go to all that trouble? You make me work very hard to hide facts that don't exist.

Isn't that Hollywood for you? Come have a drink with me afterwards, and I'll confess everything.

More lies?

Of course.

Will I be fired if I say no?

I can tell you're having too much fun with me to say "no."

I'm speechless.

Then you can't say "no."

Chapter Eight: "Shut Up, Artie!" 2

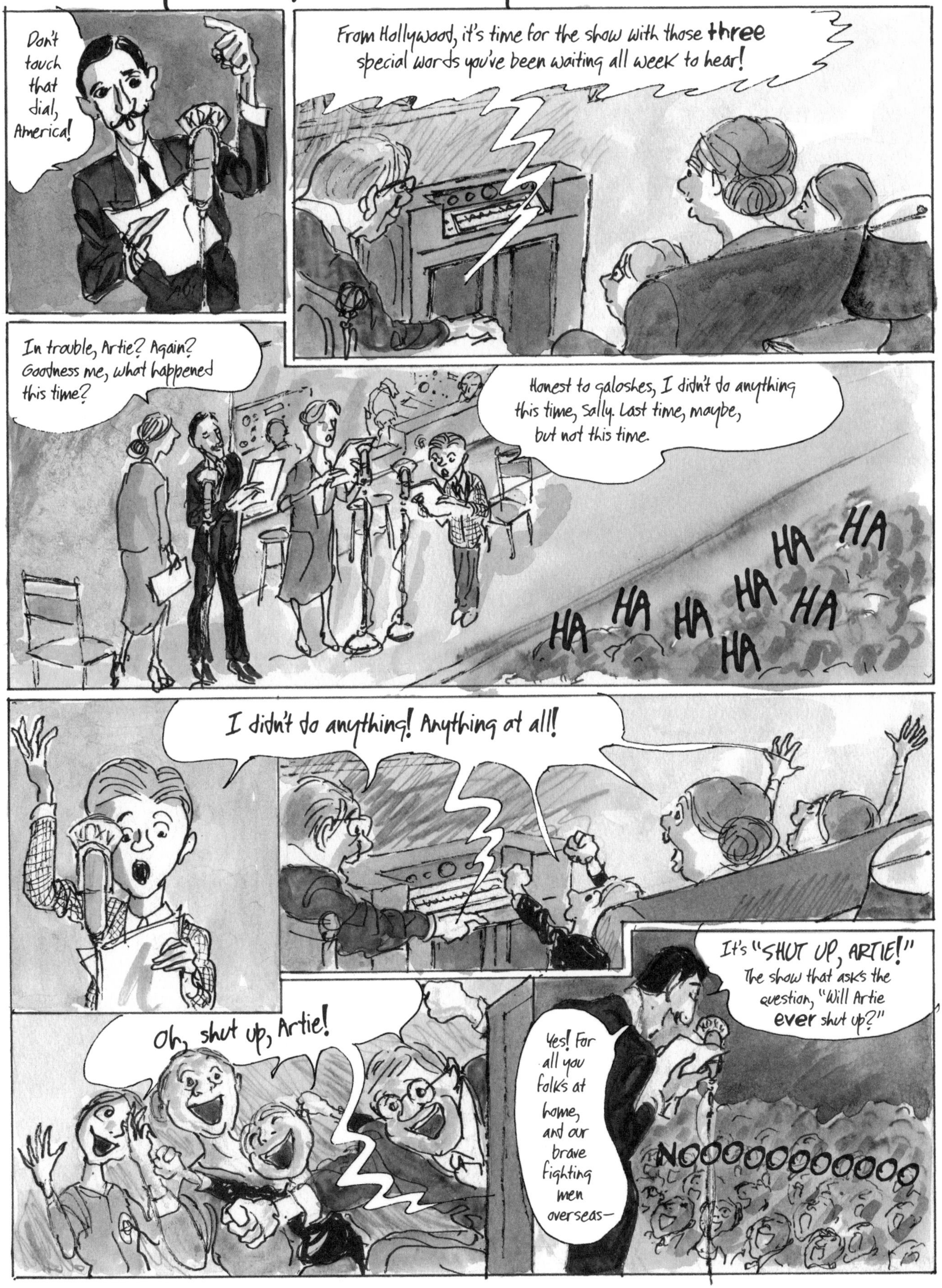
Don't touch that dial, America!
From Hollywood, it's time for the show with those three special words you've been waiting all week to hear!
In trouble, Artie? Again? Goodness me, what happened this time?
Honest to galoshes, I didn't do anything this time, Sally. Last time, maybe, but not this time.
HA HA HA HA HA HA HA HA
I didn't do anything! Anything at all!
It's "SHUT UP, ARTIE!" The show that asks the question, "Will Artie ever shut up?"
Oh, shut up, Artie!
Yes! For all you folks at home, and our brave fighting men overseas—
NOOOOOOOOOOO

Chapter Nine: Elsie's Drunk Scene

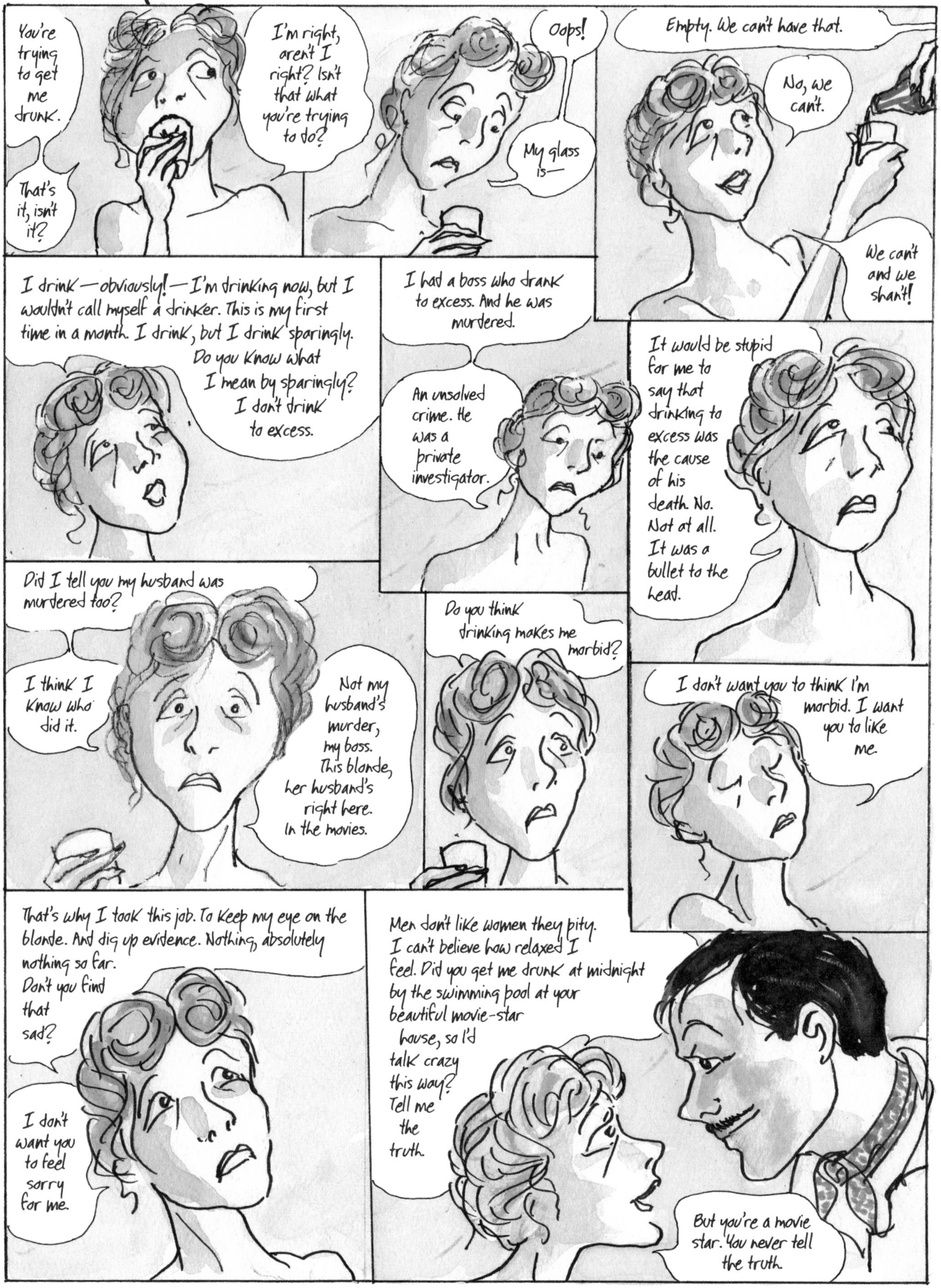

You're trying to get me drunk.
That's it, isn't it?
I'm right, aren't I right? Isn't that what you're trying to do?
Oops!
My glass is—
Empty. We can't have that.
No, we can't.
We can't and we shan't!
I drink—obviously!—I'm drinking now, but I wouldn't call myself a drinker. This is my first time in a month. I drink, but I drink sparingly.
Do you know what I mean by sparingly? I don't drink to excess.
I had a boss who drank to excess. And he was murdered.
An unsolved crime. He was a private investigator.
It would be stupid for me to say that drinking to excess was the cause of his death. No. Not at all. It was a bullet to the head.
Did I tell you my husband was murdered too?
I think I know who did it.
Not my husband's murder, my boss. This blonde, her husband's right here. In the movies.
Do you think drinking makes me morbid?
I don't want you to think I'm morbid. I want you to like me.
That's why I took this job. To keep my eye on the blonde. And dig up evidence. Nothing, absolutely nothing so far.
Don't you find that sad?
I don't want you to feel sorry for me.
Men don't like women they pity. I can't believe how relaxed I feel. Did you get me drunk at midnight by the swimming pool at your beautiful movie-star house, so I'd talk crazy this way? Tell me the truth.
But you're a movie star. You never tell the truth.

Chapter Ten: Veil Unveiled

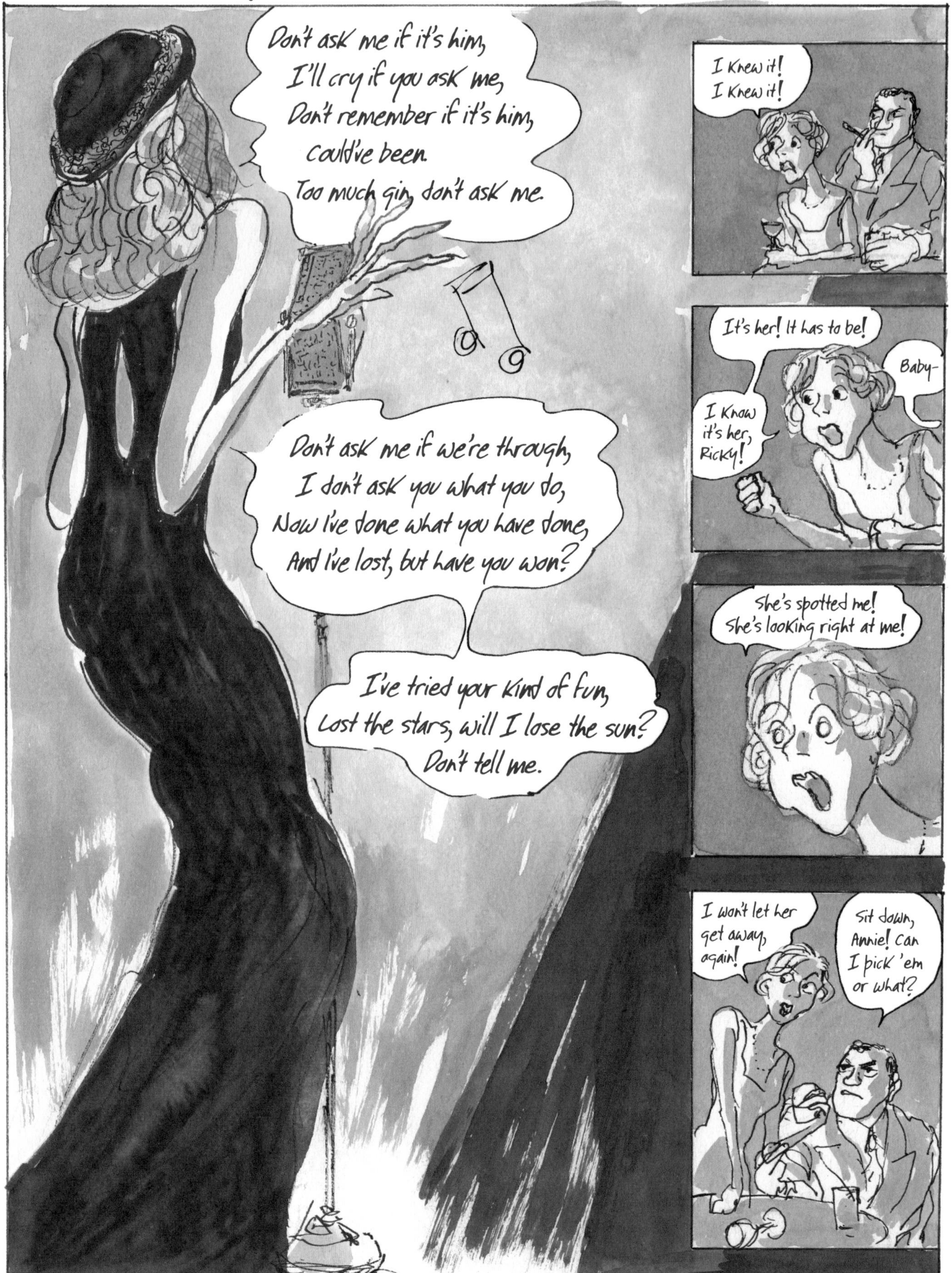

Don't ask me if it's him, I'll cry if you ask me, Don't remember if it's him, could've been. Too much gin, don't ask me.
Don't ask me if we're through, I don't ask you what you do, Now I've done what you have done, And I've lost, but have you won?
I've tried your kind of fun, Lost the stars, will I lose the sun? Don't tell me.
I knew it! I knew it!
It's her! It has to be!
Baby-
I know it's her, Ricky!
She's spotted me! She's looking right at me!
I won't let her get away, again!
Sit down, Annie! Can I pick 'em or what?

87

Chapter Eleven: Anything You Want

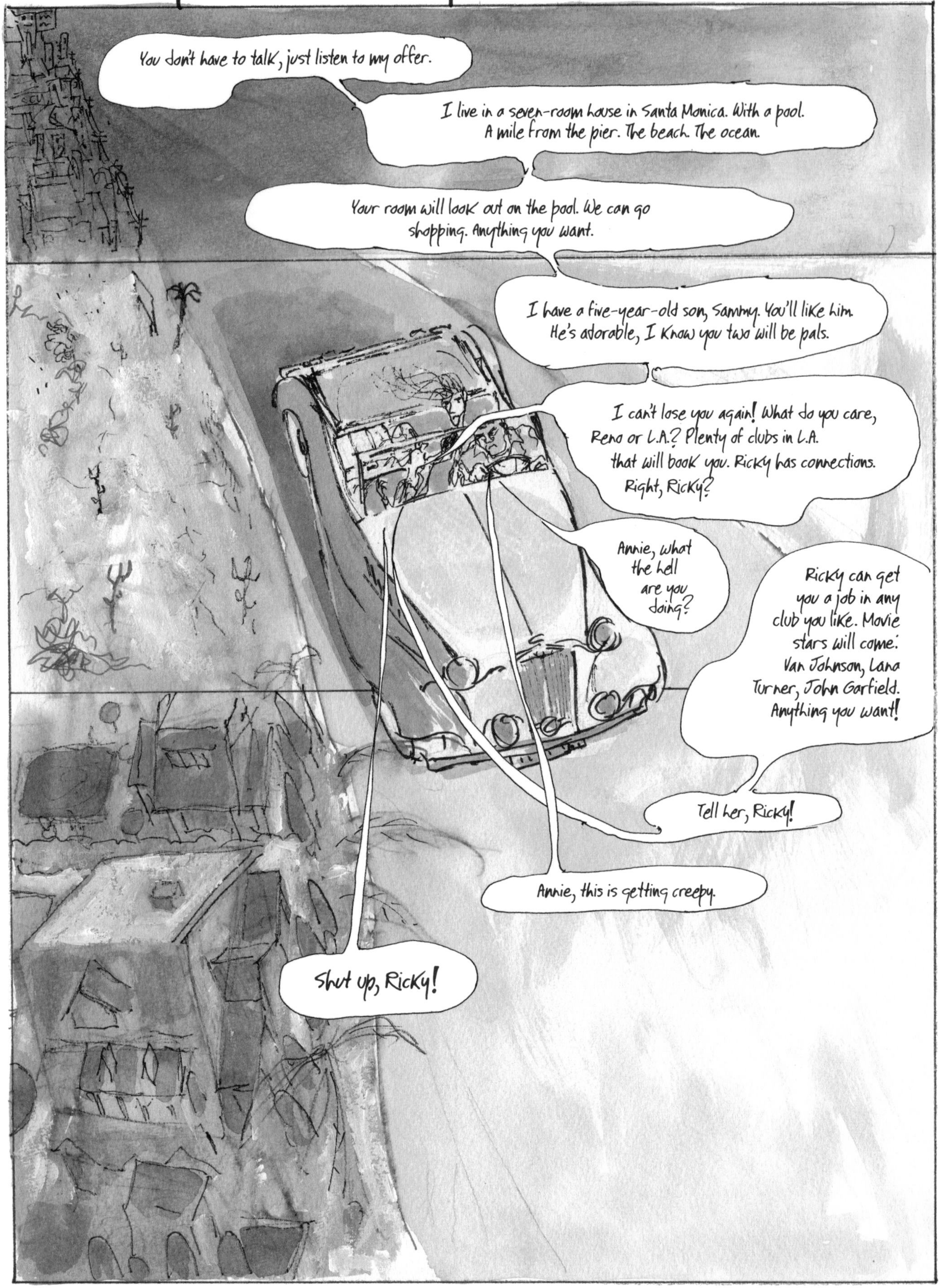

You don't have to talk, just listen to my offer.
I live in a seven-room house in Santa Monica. With a pool. A mile from the pier. The beach. The ocean.
Your room will look out on the pool. We can go shopping. Anything you want.
I have a five-year-old son, Sammy. You'll like him. He's adorable, I know you two will be pals.
I can't lose you again! What do you care, Reno or L.A.? Plenty of clubs in L.A. that will book you. Ricky has connections. Right, Ricky?
Annie, what the hell are you doing?
Ricky can get you a job in any club you like. Movie stars will come: Van Johnson, Lana Turner, John Garfield. Anything you want!
Tell her, Ricky!
Annie, this is getting creepy.
Shut up, Ricky!

Chapter Twelve: Tiny Tim

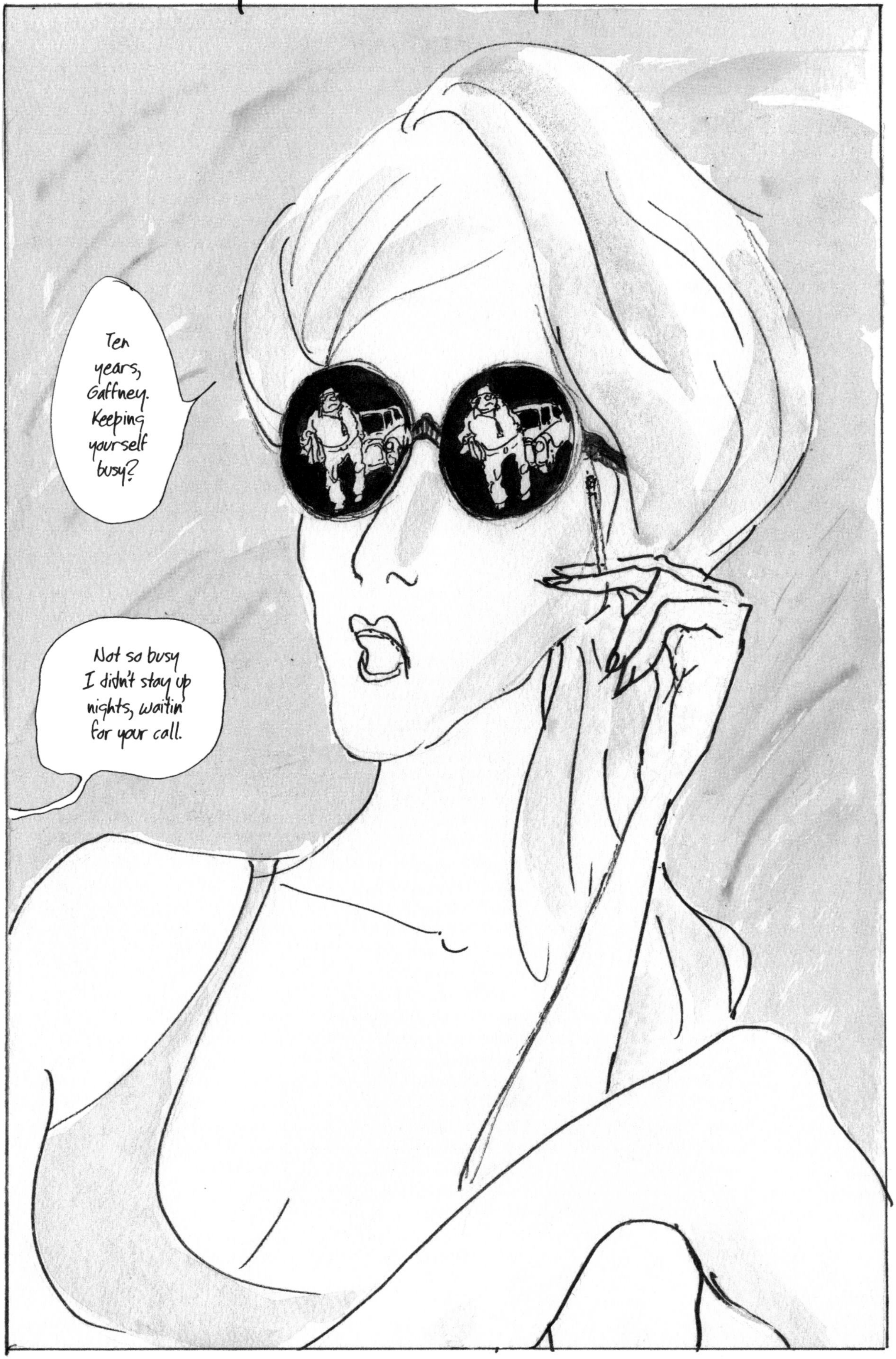
Ten years, Gaffney. Keeping yourself busy?
Not so busy I didn't stay up nights, waitin' for your call.

90

Chapter Thirteen: The Kiss-Off

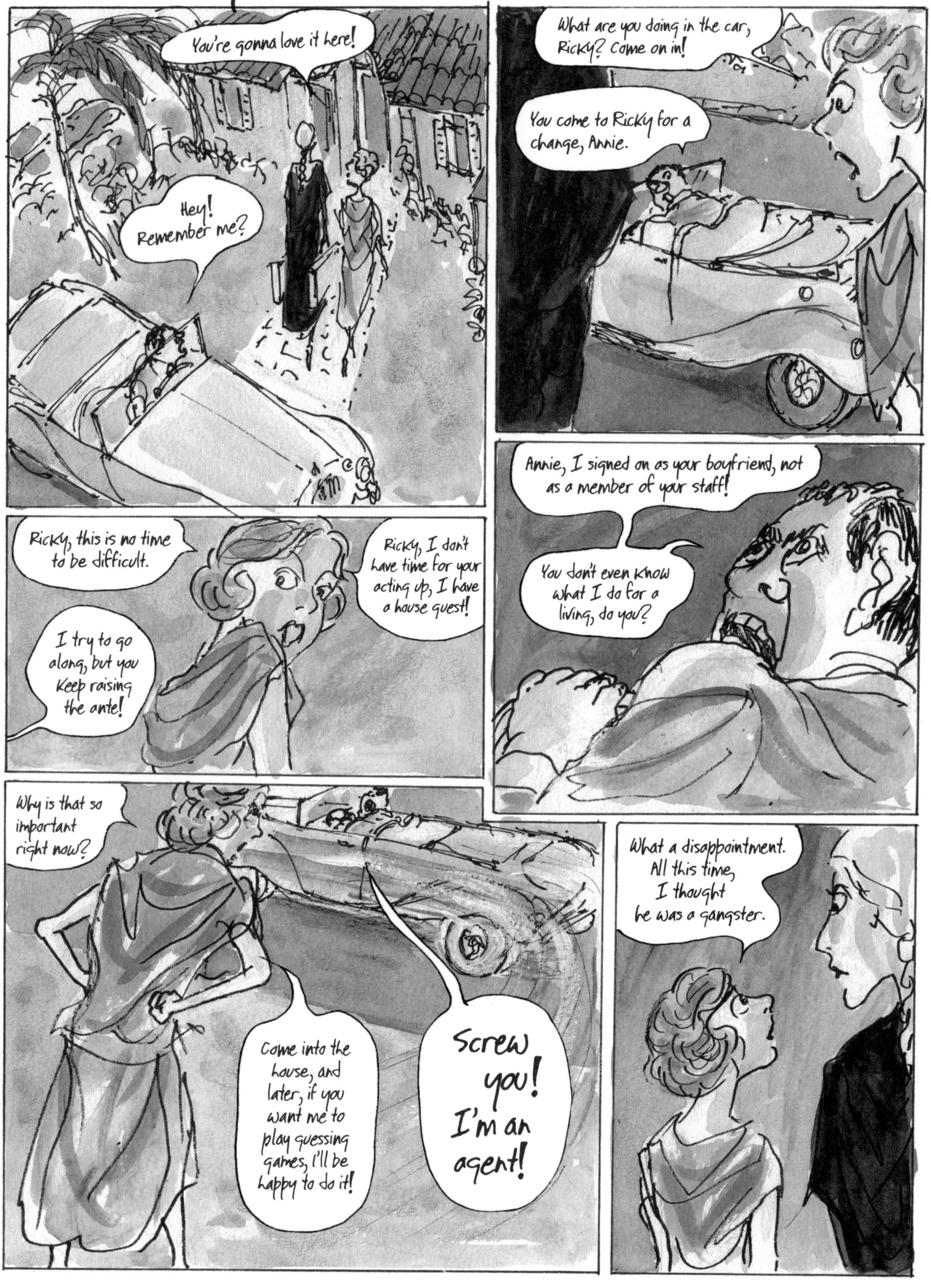

You're gonna love it here!
Hey! Remember me?
What are you doing in the car, Ricky? Come on in!
You come to Ricky for a change, Annie.
Annie, I signed on as your boyfriend, not as a member of your staff!
You don't even know what I do for a living, do you?
Ricky, this is no time to be difficult.
Ricky, I don't have time for your acting up, I have a house guest!
I try to go along, but you keep raising the ante!
Why is that so important right now?
Come into the house, and later, if you want me to play guessing games, I'll be happy to do it!
Screw you! I'm an agent!
What a disappointment. All this time, I thought he was a gangster.

Chapter Fourteen: Dressed to Kill

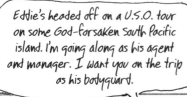

Eddie's headed off on a U.S.O. tour on some God-forsaken South Pacific island. I'm going along as his agent and manager. I want you on the trip as his bodyguard.

Whadaya think?

Another star on the trip is Hugh Patton. He's hot right now. He's up for the lead in a film Eddie wants real bad. You've seen him?

I don't go to pictures.

My Eddie and Hugh Patton hit this town the same time. You know Eddie, he's a party boy, an open book. But Hugh Patton he doesn't socialize. Doesn't go to parties. I've never met him. He's a mystery man. The rumor is he's a pansy.

In three weeks, we go off on the tour. Before then, let's see what you come up with. Photos, affidavits, stuff we can take to the newspapers. So before Elsie Hannigan gets a chance to kill the story, it's bye-bye Hugh Patton. And Eddie gets the part.

What if he's not queer? Or I can't prove it?

Then off we go to entertain the boys. Into a war zone. Where accidents happen. Hugh Patton's a big, big guy. An easy target for some sniper in the jungle. Not a fatal wound. Just bad enough to keep him out of action six months, a year.

Almost tragic, when you think about it. But it's all for Eddie, Eddie gets what he wants.

And I get...?

15,000 down front, another 35,000 when the job is done.

Makes me feel good that we're friends again, Mae.

Chapter Fifteen: A Song for Sammy

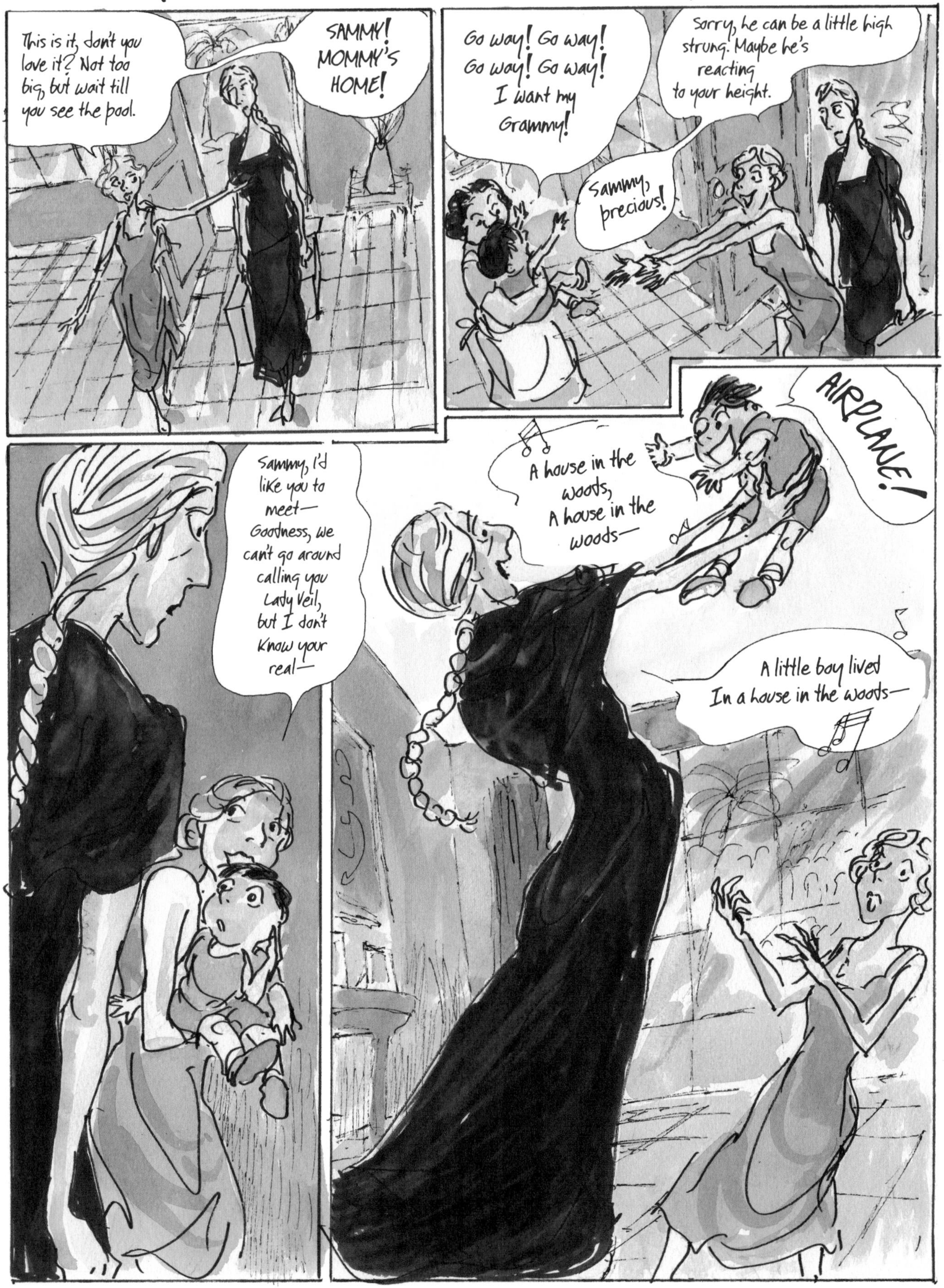

This is it, don't you love it? Not too big, but wait till you see the pool.
SAMMY! MOMMY'S HOME!
Go way! Go way! Go way! Go way! I want my Grammy!
Sorry, he can be a little high strung. Maybe he's reacting to your height.
Sammy, precious!
Sammy, I'd like you to meet— Goodness, we can't go around calling you Lady Veil, but I don't know your real—
A house in the woods, A house in the woods—
AIRPLANE!
A little boy lived In a house in the woods—

95

Chapter Sixteen: Something for the Boys

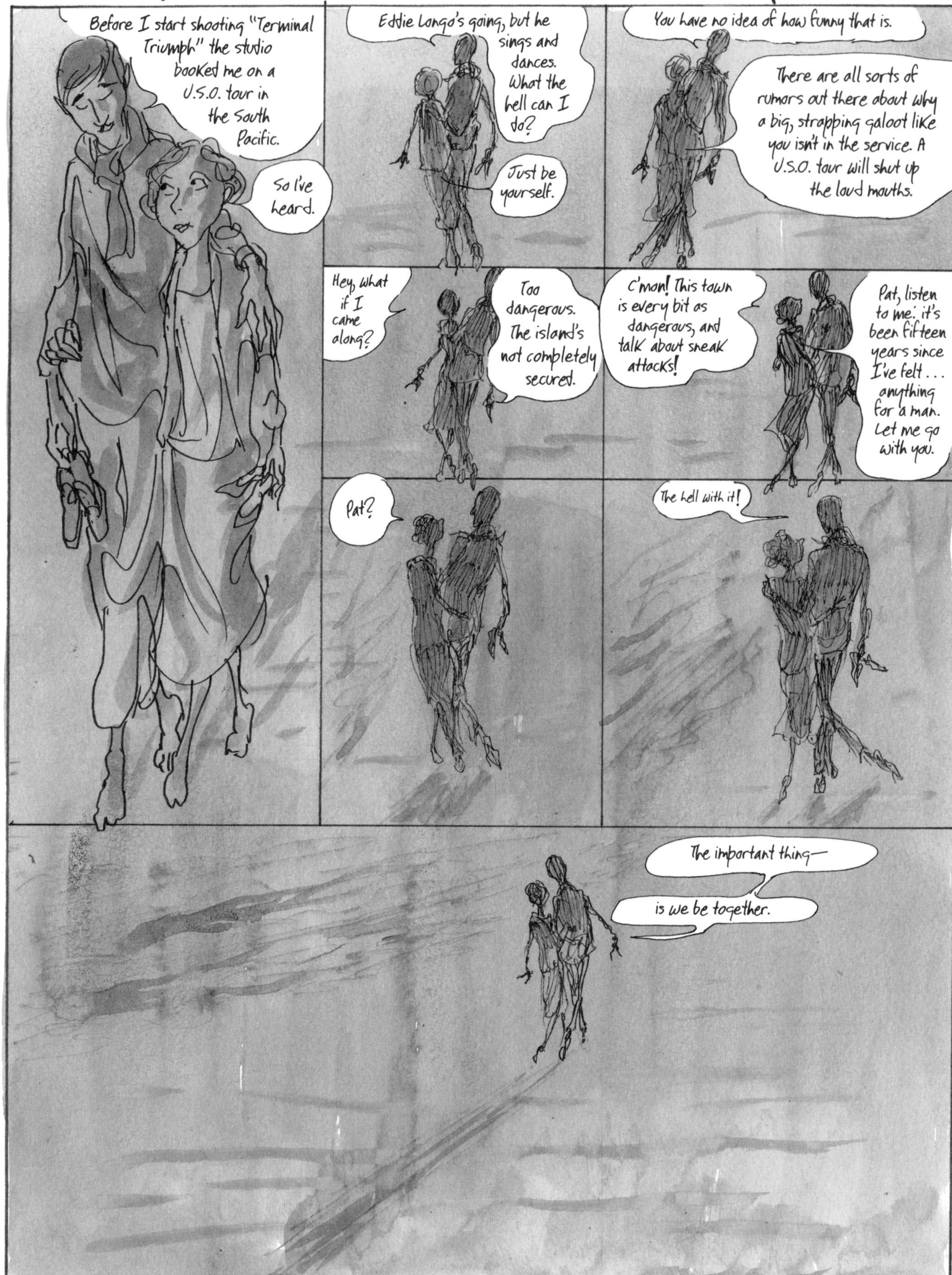

Before I start shooting "Terminal Triumph" the studio booked me on a U.S.O. tour in the South Pacific.
So I've heard.
Eddie Longo's going, but he sings and dances. What the hell can I do?
Just be yourself.
You have no idea of how funny that is.
There are all sorts of rumors out there about why a big, strapping galoot like you isn't in the service. A U.S.O. tour will shut up the loud mouths.
Hey, what if I came along?
Too dangerous. The island's not completely secured.
C'mon! This town is every bit as dangerous, and talk about sneak attacks!
Pat, listen to me: it's been fifteen years since I've felt . . . anything for a man. Let me go with you.
Pat?
The hell with it!
The important thing—
is we be together.

Chapter Seventeen: The Ride to the Airport

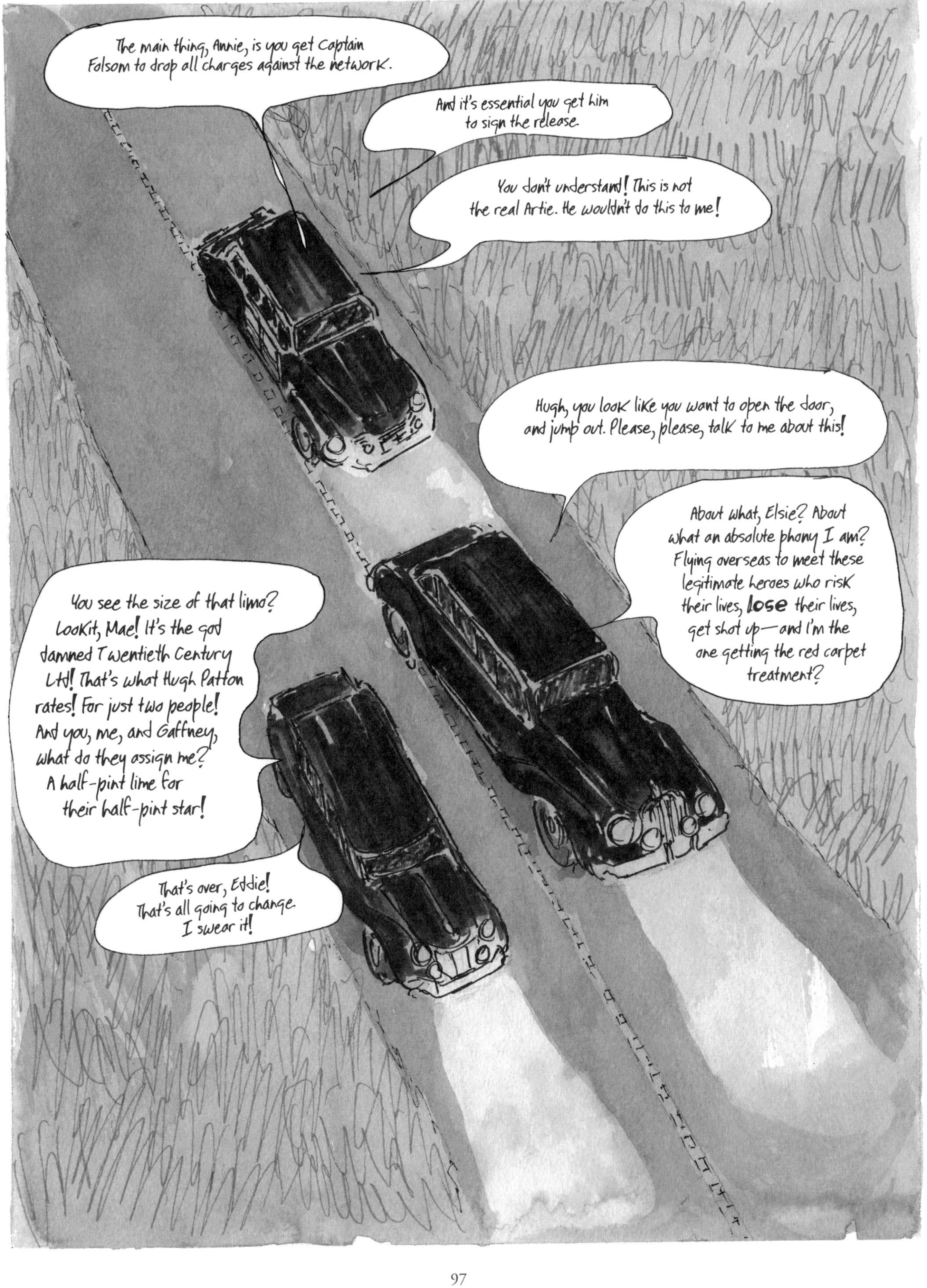
The main thing, Annie, is you get Captain Folsom to drop all charges against the network.
And it's essential you get him to sign the release.
You don't understand! This is not the real Artie. He wouldn't do this to me!
Hugh, you look like you want to open the door, and jump out. Please, please, talk to me about this!
About what, Elsie? About what an absolute phony I am? Flying overseas to meet these legitimate heroes who risk their lives, **lose** their lives, get shot up—and I'm the one getting the red carpet treatment?
You see the size of that limo? LooKit, Mae! It's the god damned Twentieth Century Ltd! That's what Hugh Patton rates! For just two people! And you, me, and Gaffney, what do they assign me? A half-pint limo for their half-pint star!
That's over, Eddie! That's all going to change. I swear it!

Chapter Eighteen: Artie's War

Men, you can see behind me this stage being constructed. It's for the U.S.O. performers who are flying out from Hollywood to entertain our troops here on Tarawa. These actors and singers and dancers don't know what might be facing them when they get here. If they did, they might cancel the trip.

Now Tarawa has been secured, but there are still pockets of resistance—diehards—hiding out in the jungle, and they have more places to hide than we know where to look for them. We can't let them get away with that, can we?

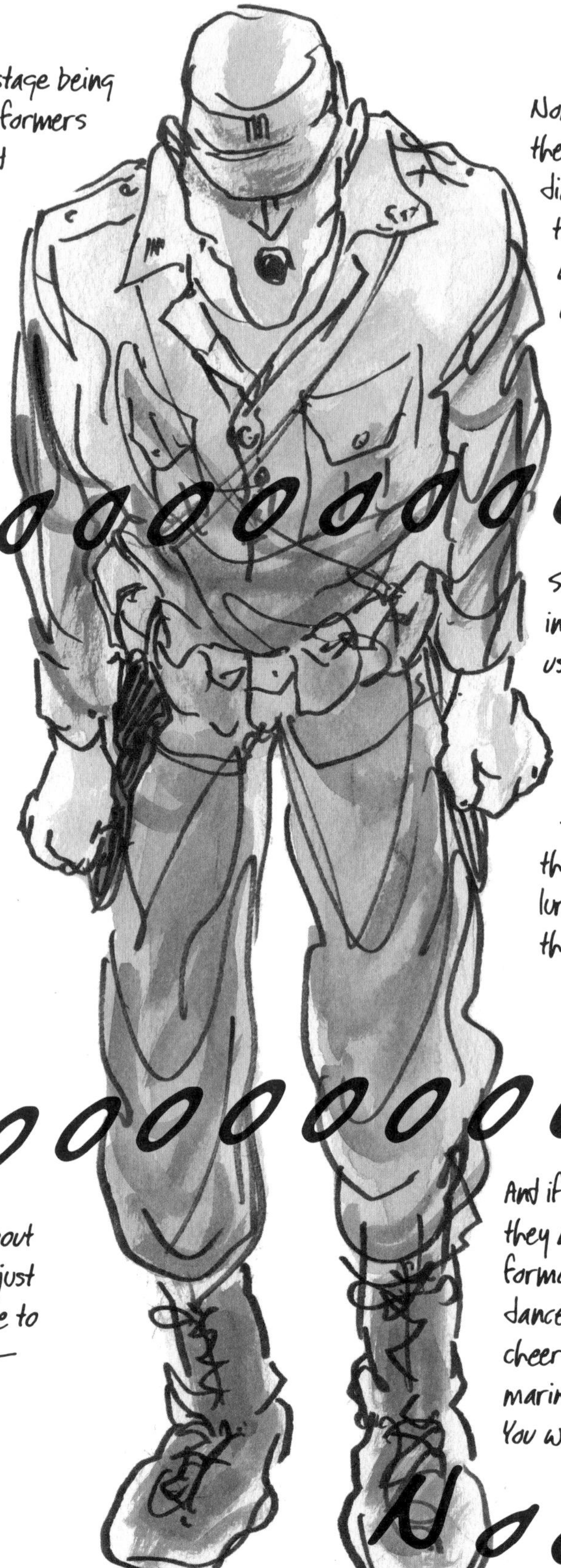

Nooooooooooo!

Right, the show must go on. You men have fought hard and won hard, and now it's your right to get a look or two at some of these Hollywood stars—some of them of draft age who somehow—for some reason—were never called up to serve their country.

So that's where this plan of mine comes in. I don't have official permission for us to act on it. You'll all have to volunteer, I can't order you to sit in the audience tomorrow night, enjoying the show like you don't have a worry in the world. Laughing, applauding—with the enemy out there—these diehards lurking in the jungle—**also** watching the show—

Booooooooo!

Yeah, I bet they feel just awful about it. So I came up with a plan to—just maybe—give these boys a chance to experience—maybe, just maybe—what you leathernecks have been going through.

And if they're out there—and my guess is they won't be able to resist this U.S.O. performance: a brightly lit stage, singers and dancers right there in the spotlight, and a cheering, applauding audience of unprepared marines . . . what they'll see is sitting ducks! You will all be sitting ducks!

Nooooo!

Chapter Nineteen: Plane Talk

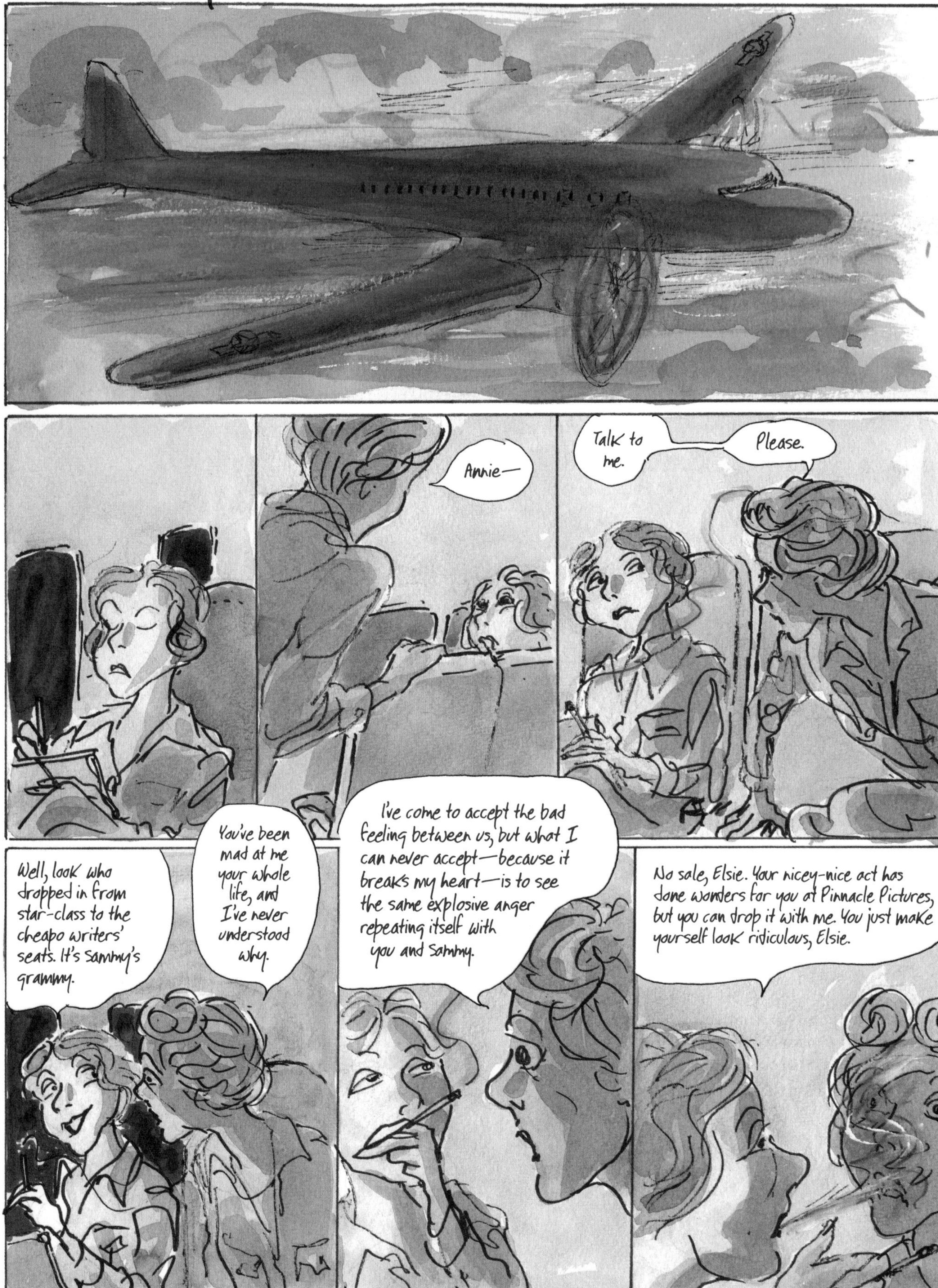

Annie—
Talk to me.
Please.
Well, look who dropped in from star-class to the cheapo writers' seats. It's Sammy's grammy.
You've been mad at me your whole life, and I've never understood why.
I've come to accept the bad feeling between us, but what I can never accept—because it breaks my heart—is to see the same explosive anger repeating itself with you and Sammy.
No sale, Elsie. Your nicey-nice act has done wonders for you at Pinnacle Pictures, but you can drop it with me. You just make yourself look ridiculous, Elsie.

Chapter Twenty: The Island

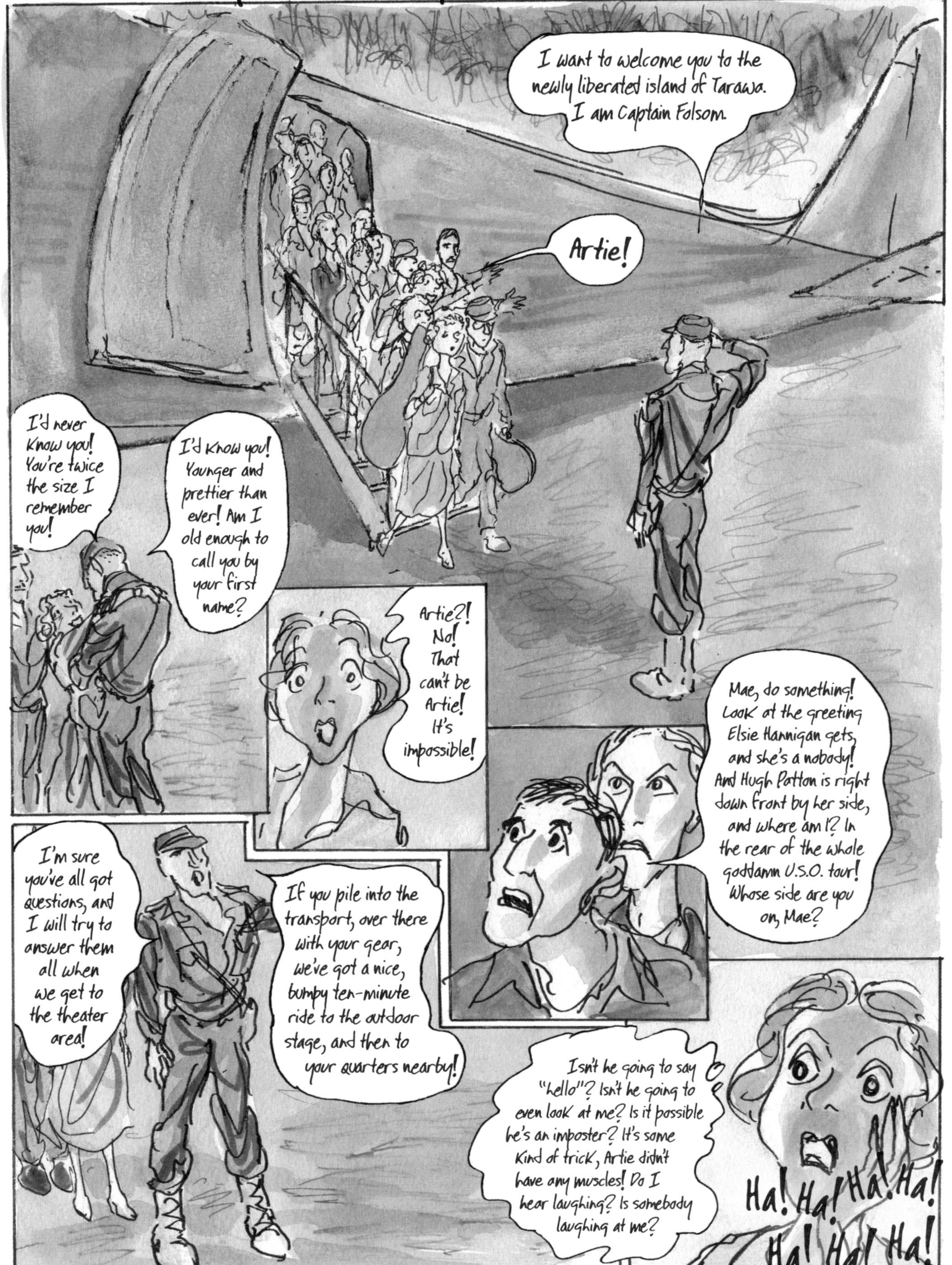
I want to welcome you to the newly liberated island of Tarawa. I am Captain Folsom.
Artie!
I'd never know you! You're twice the size I remember you!
I'd know you! Younger and prettier than ever! Am I old enough to call you by your first name?
Artie?! No! That can't be Artie! It's impossible!
Mae, do something! Look at the greeting Elsie Hannigan gets, and she's a nobody! And Hugh Patton is right down front by her side, and where am I? In the rear of the whole goddamn U.S.O. tour! Whose side are you on, Mae?
I'm sure you've all got questions, and I will try to answer them all when we get to the theater area!
If you pile into the transport, over there with your gear, we've got a nice, bumpy ten-minute ride to the outdoor stage, and then to your quarters nearby!
Isn't he going to say "hello"? Isn't he going to even look at me? Is it possible he's an imposter? It's some kind of trick, Artie didn't have any muscles! Do I hear laughing? Is somebody laughing at me?
Ha! Ha! Ha! Ha! Ha! Ha! Ha!

Chapter Twenty-One: The Audience

Chapter Twenty-Two: The Jungle Follies

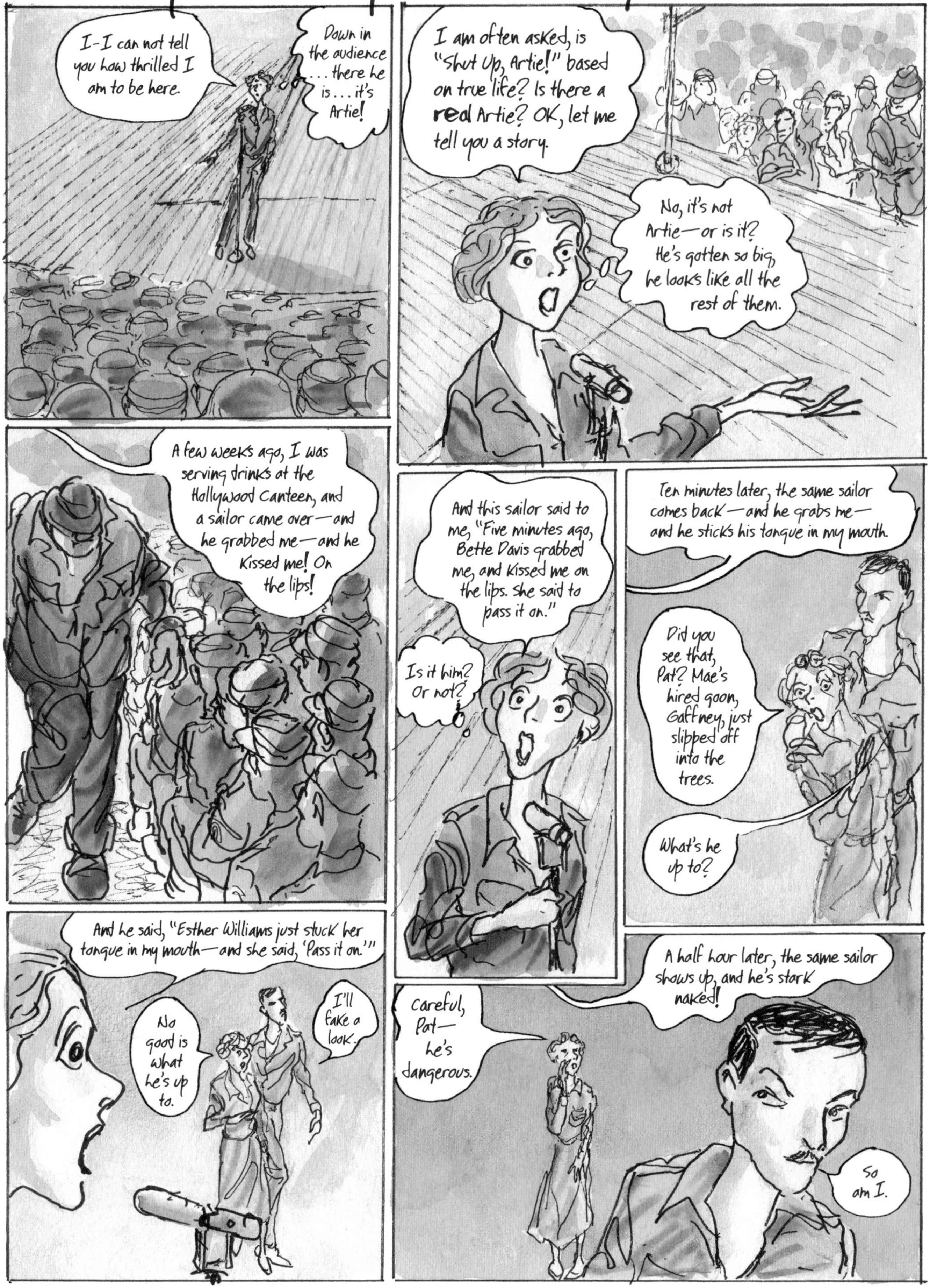

I-I can not tell you how thrilled I am to be here.
Down in the audience . . . there he is . . . it's Artie!
I am often asked, is "Shut Up, Artie!" based on true life? Is there a real Artie? OK, let me tell you a story.
No, it's not Artie—or is it? He's gotten so big, he looks like all the rest of them.
A few weeks ago, I was serving drinks at the Hollywood Canteen, and a sailor came over—and he grabbed me—and he kissed me! On the lips!
And this sailor said to me, "Five minutes ago, Bette Davis grabbed me, and kissed me on the lips. She said to pass it on."
Is it him? Or not?
Ten minutes later, the same sailor comes back—and he grabs me—and he sticks his tongue in my mouth.
Did you see that, Pat? Mae's hired goon, Gaffney, just slipped off into the trees.
What's he up to?
And he said, "Esther Williams just stuck her tongue in my mouth—and she said, 'Pass it on.'"
No good is what he's up to.
I'll take a look.
A half hour later, the same sailor shows up, and he's stark naked!
Careful, Pat—he's dangerous.
So am I.

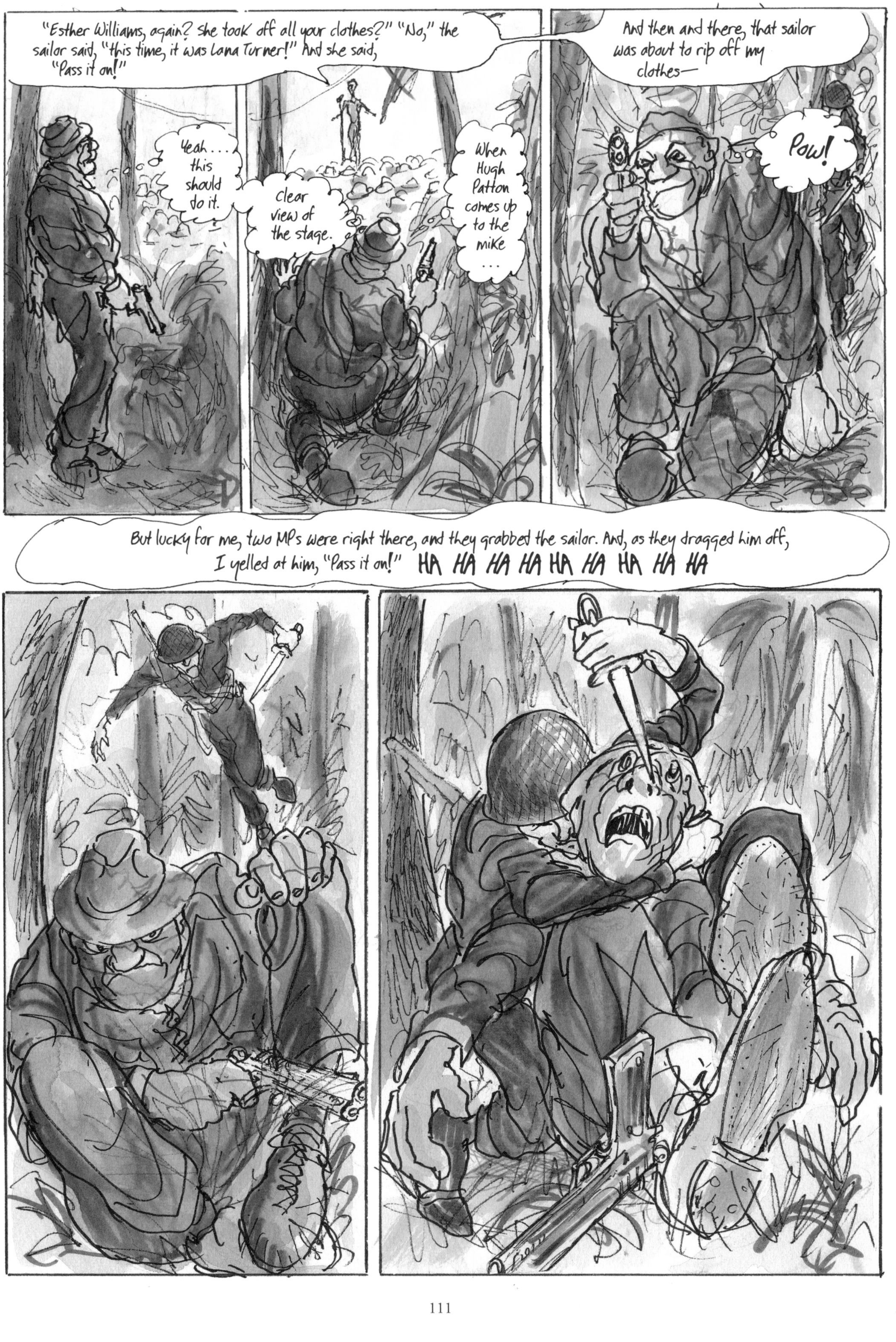
"Esther Williams, again? she took off all your clothes?" "No," the sailor said, "this time, it was Lana Turner!" And she said, "Pass it on!"
And then and there, that sailor was about to rip off my clothes—
Yeah . . . this should do it.
Clear view of the stage.
When Hugh Patton comes up to the mike . . .
Pow!
But lucky for me, two MPs were right there, and they grabbed the sailor. And, as they dragged him off, I yelled at him, "Pass it on!" HA HA HA HA HA HA HA HA HA

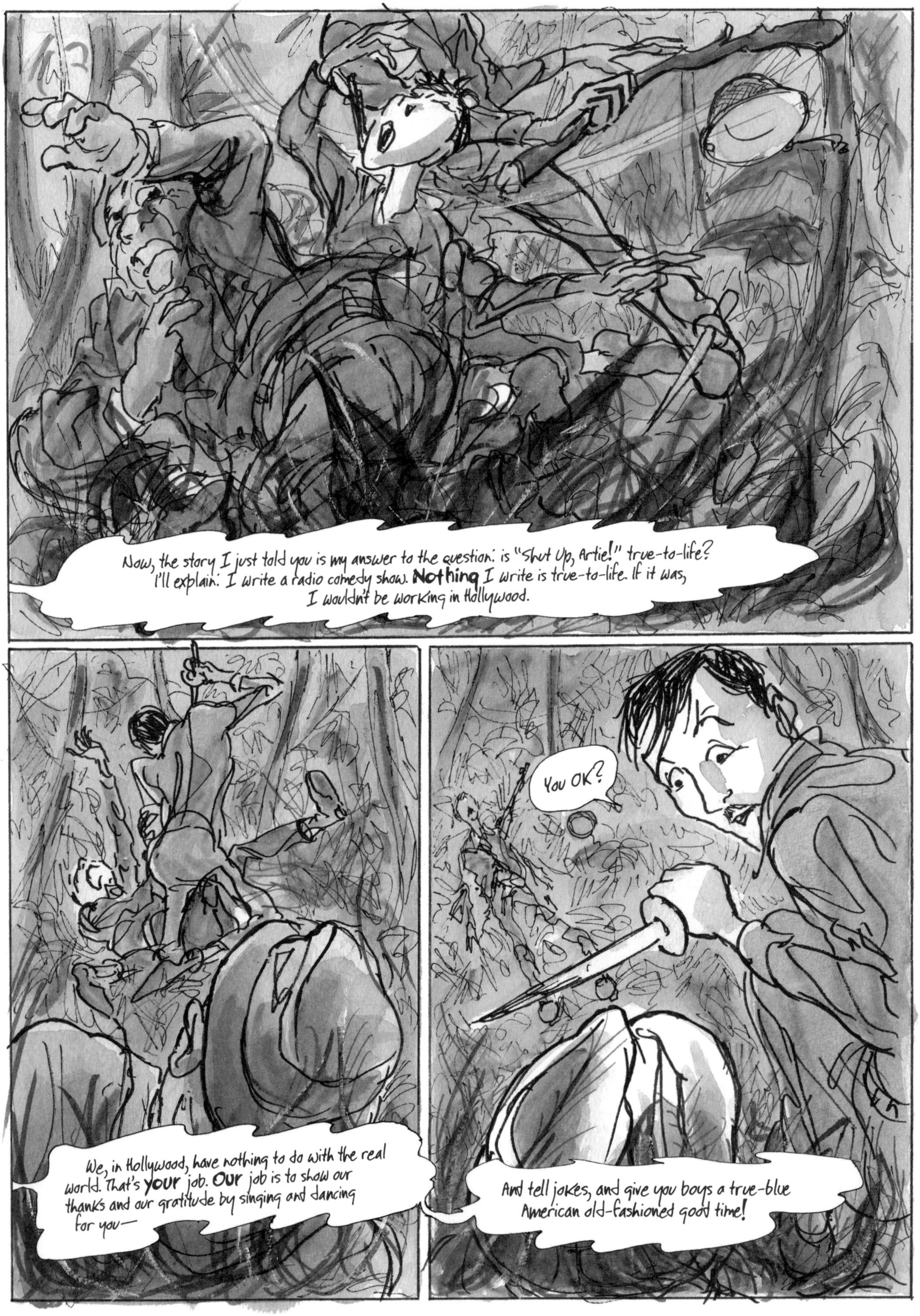

Now, the story I just told you is my answer to the question: is "Shut Up, Artie!" true-to-life? I'll explain: I write a radio comedy show. Nothing I write is true-to-life. If it was, I wouldn't be working in Hollywood.
We, in Hollywood, have nothing to do with the real world. That's your job. Our job is to show our thanks and our gratitude by singing and dancing for you—
You OK?
And tell jokes, and give you boys a true-blue American old-fashioned good time!

114

115

116

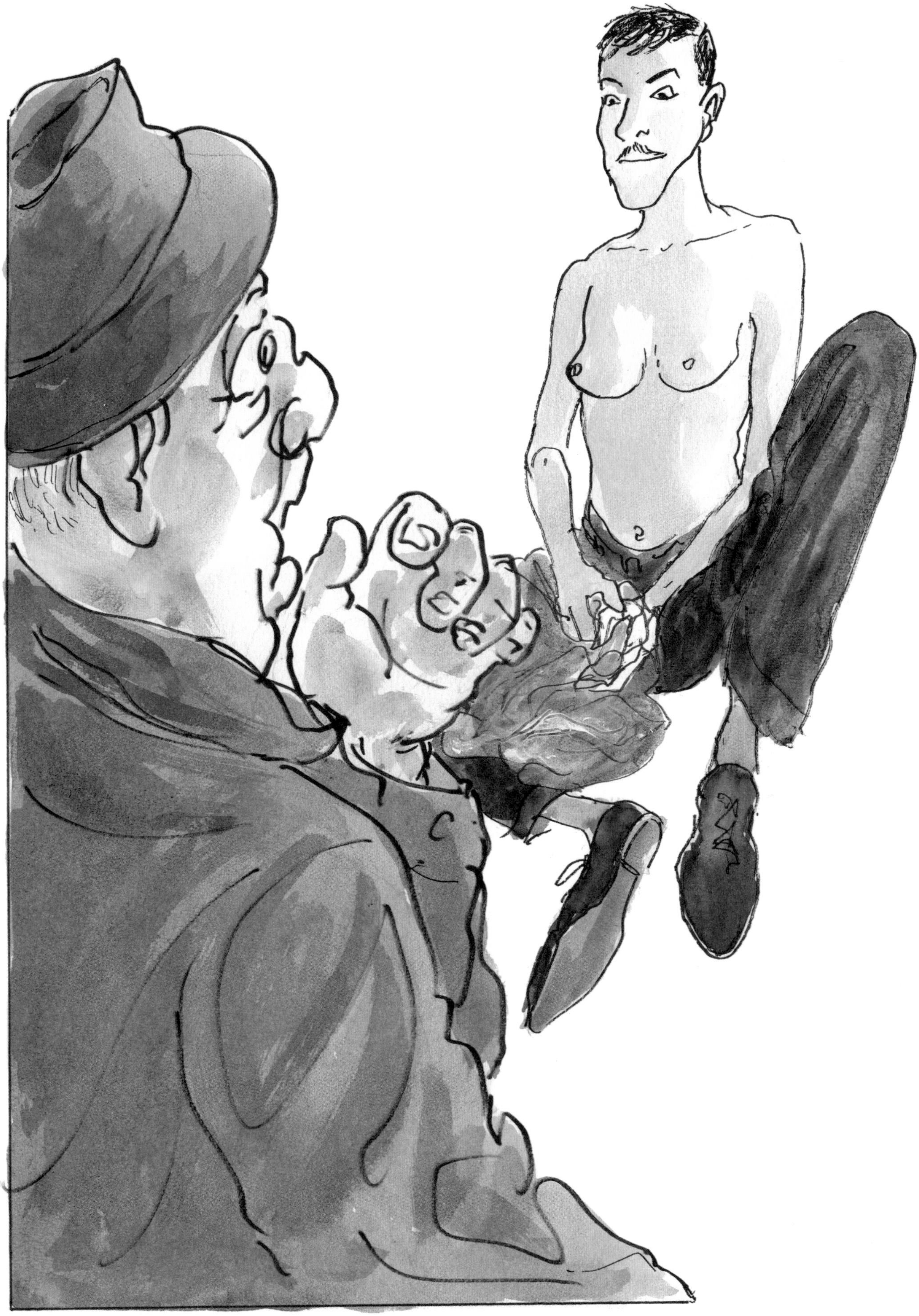

118

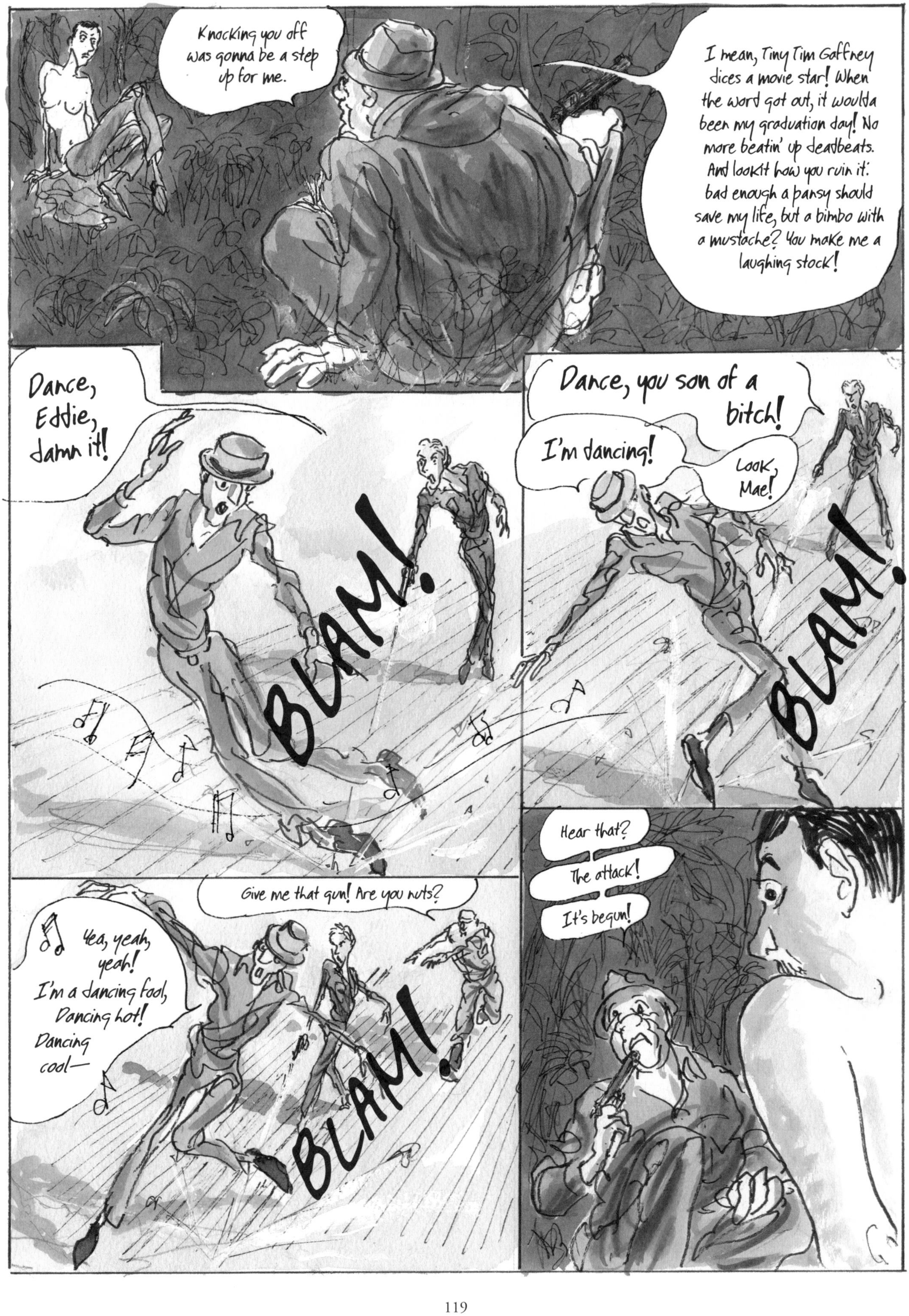
Knocking you off was gonna be a step up for me.
I mean, Tiny Tim Gaffney dices a movie star! When the word got out, it woulda been my graduation day! No more beatin' up deadbeats. And lookit how you ruin it: bad enough a pansy should save my life, but a bimbo with a mustache? You make me a laughing stock!
Dance, Eddie, damn it!
BLAM!
Dance, you son of a bitch!
I'm dancing!
Look, Mae!
BLAM!
Give me that gun! Are you nuts?
Yea, yeah, yeah! I'm a dancing fool, Dancing hot! Dancing cool—
BLAM!
Hear that?
The attack!
It's begun!

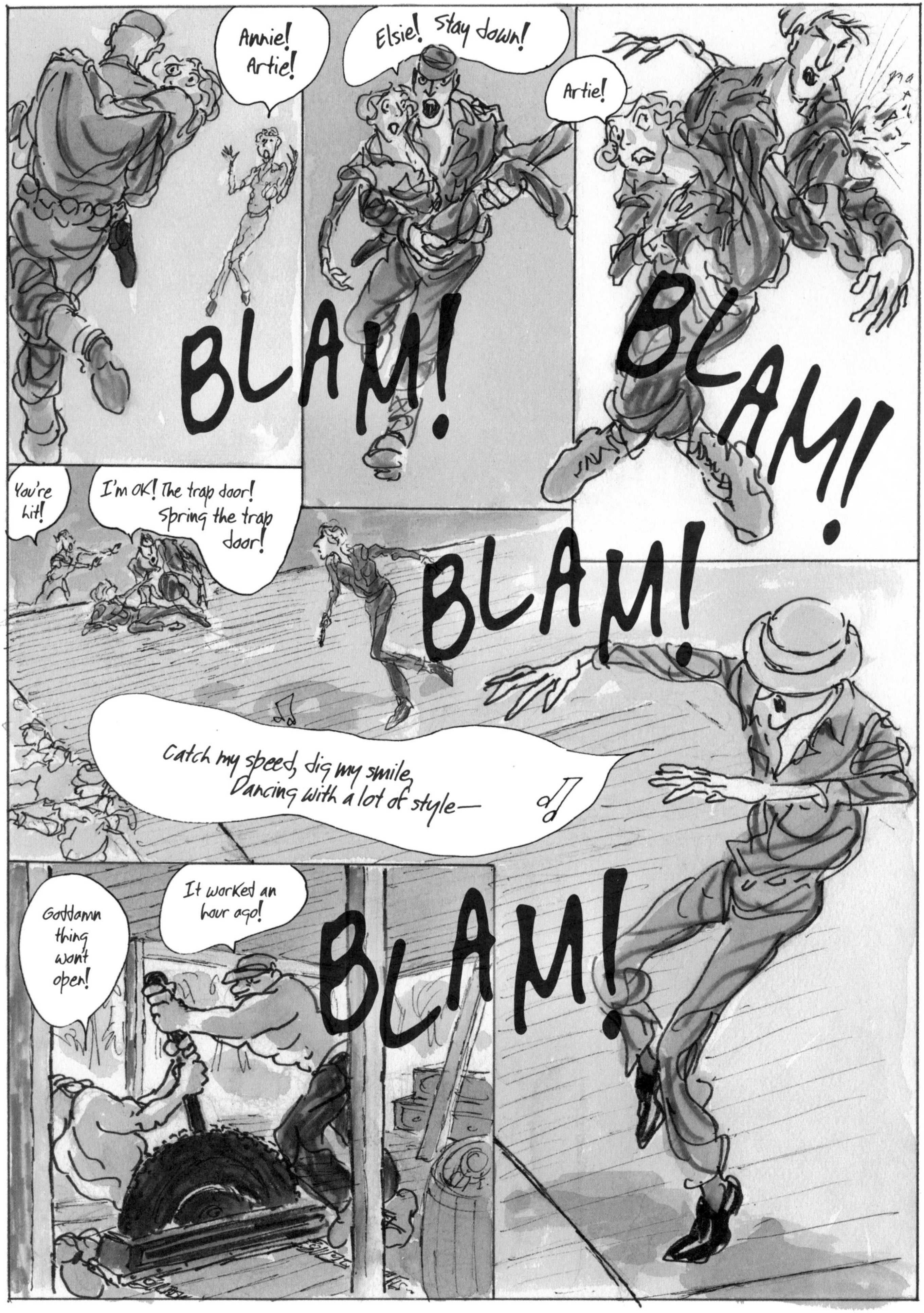
Annie! Artie!
Elsie! Stay down!
Artie!
BLAM!
BLAM!
BLAM!
You're hit!
I'm OK! The trap door! Spring the trap door!
BLAM!
Catch my speed, dig my smile,
Dancing with a lot of style—
Goddamn thing won't open!
It worked an hour ago!
BLAM!

123

125

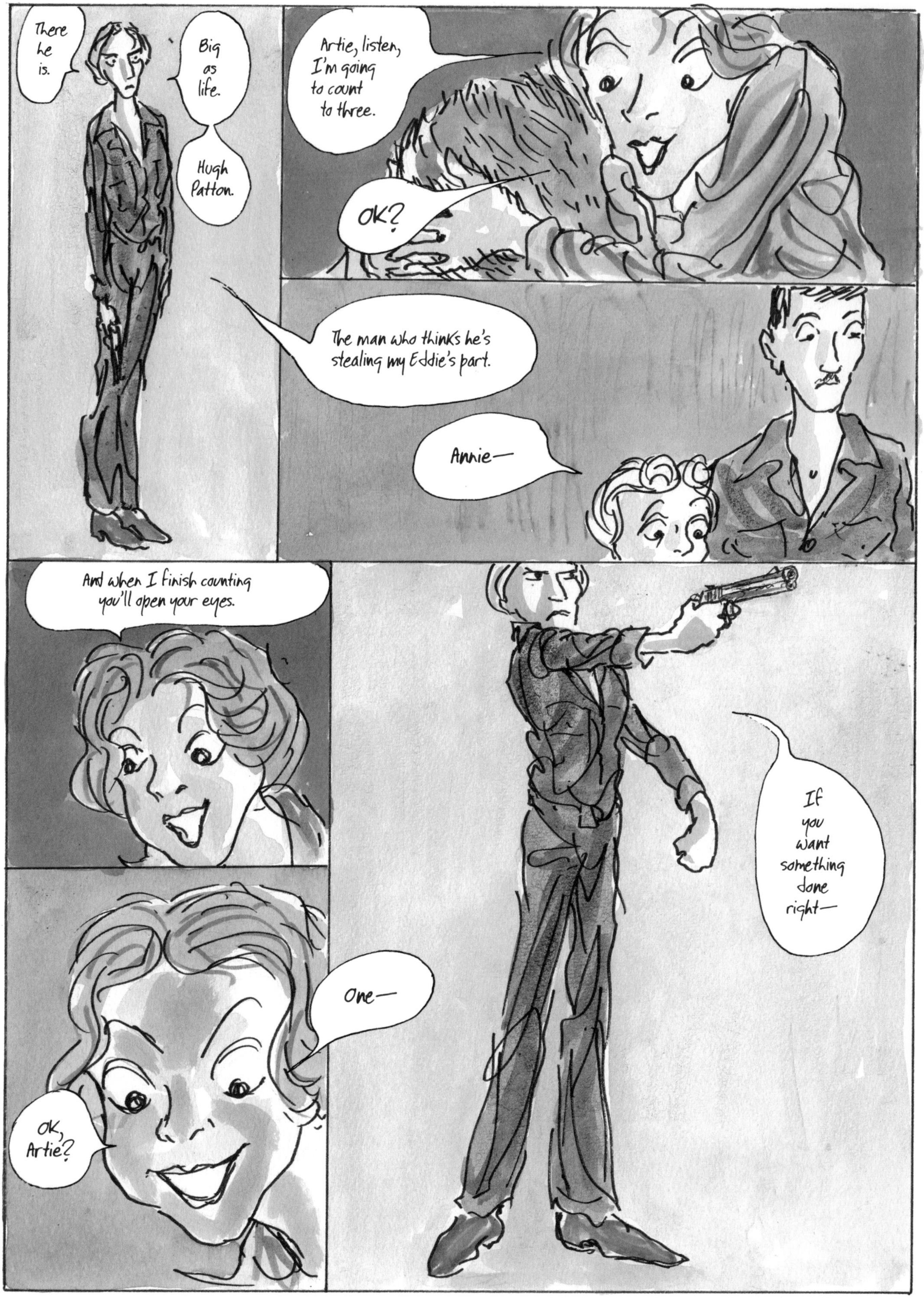
There he is.
Big as life.
Hugh Patton.
Artie, listen, I'm going to count to three.
OK?
The man who thinks he's stealing my Eddie's part.
Annie—
And when I finish counting you'll open your eyes.
If you want something done right—
One—
OK, Artie?

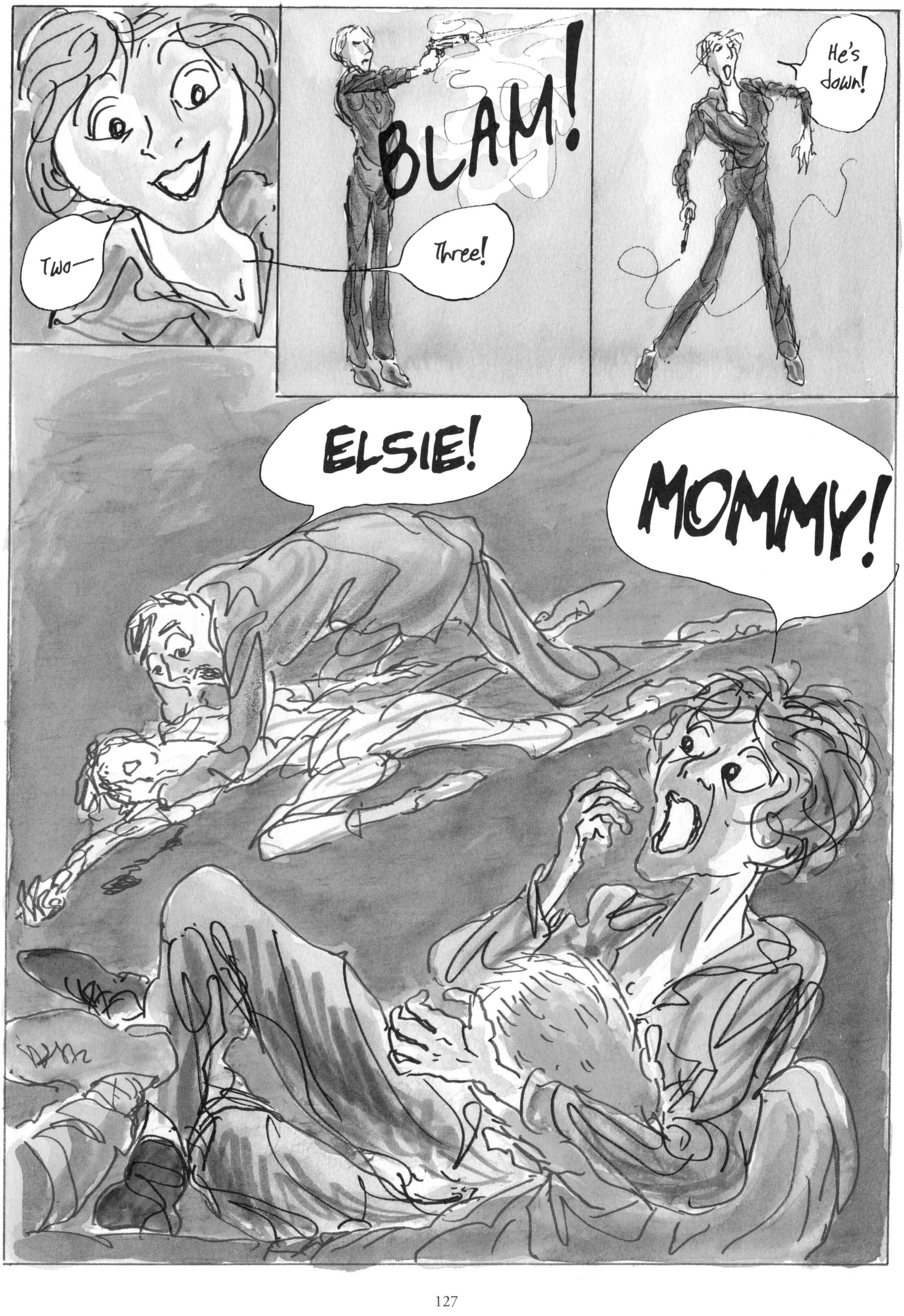

Two—
Three!
BLAM!
He's down!
ELSIE!
MOMMY!

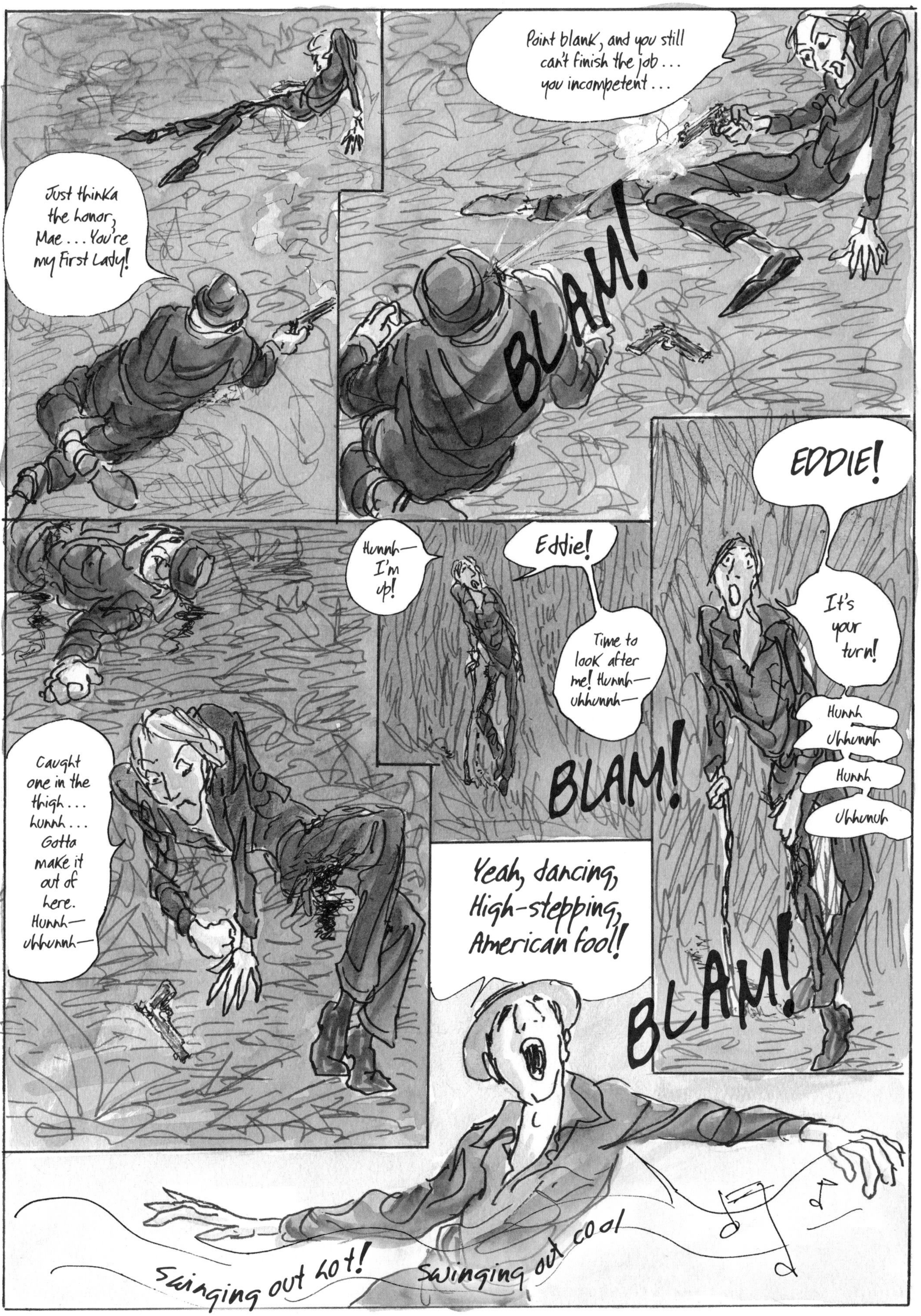
Just thinka the honor, Mae . . . You're my First Lady!
Point blank, and you still can't finish the job . . . you incompetent . . .
BLAM!
Caught one in the thigh . . . hunnh . . . Gotta make it out of here. Hunnh— uhhunnh—
Hunnh— I'm up!
Eddie!
Time to look after me! Hunnh— uhhunnh—
BLAM!
EDDIE!
It's your turn!
Hunnh
Uhhunnh
Hunnh
Uhhunuh
BLAM!
Yeah, dancing, High-stepping, American fool!
Swinging out hot! Swinging out cool

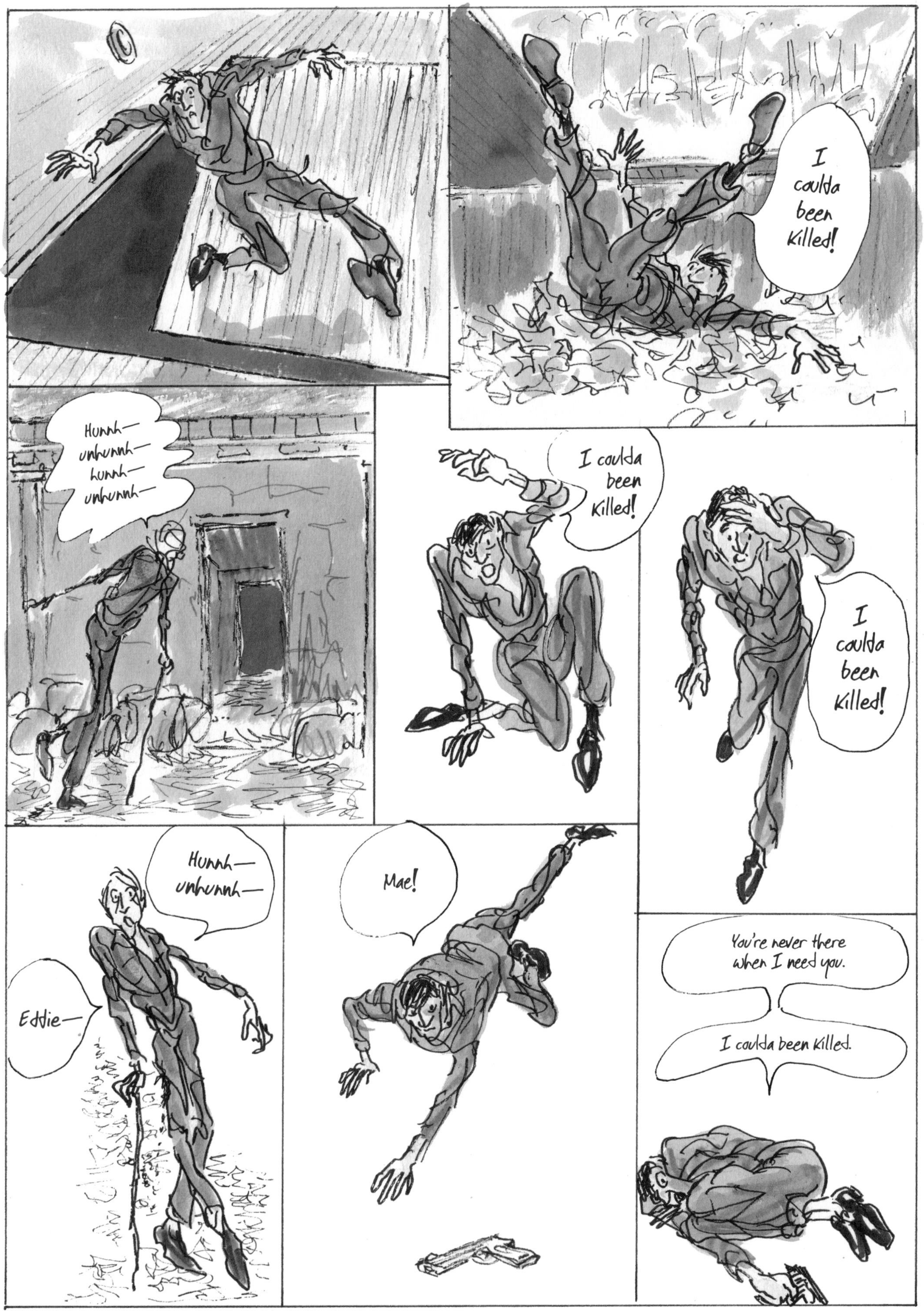
I coulda been Killed!
Hunnh—unhunnh—hunnh—unhunnh—
I coulda been Killed!
I coulda been Killed!
Hunnh—unhunnh—
Eddie—
Mae!
You're never there when I need you.
I coulda been Killed.

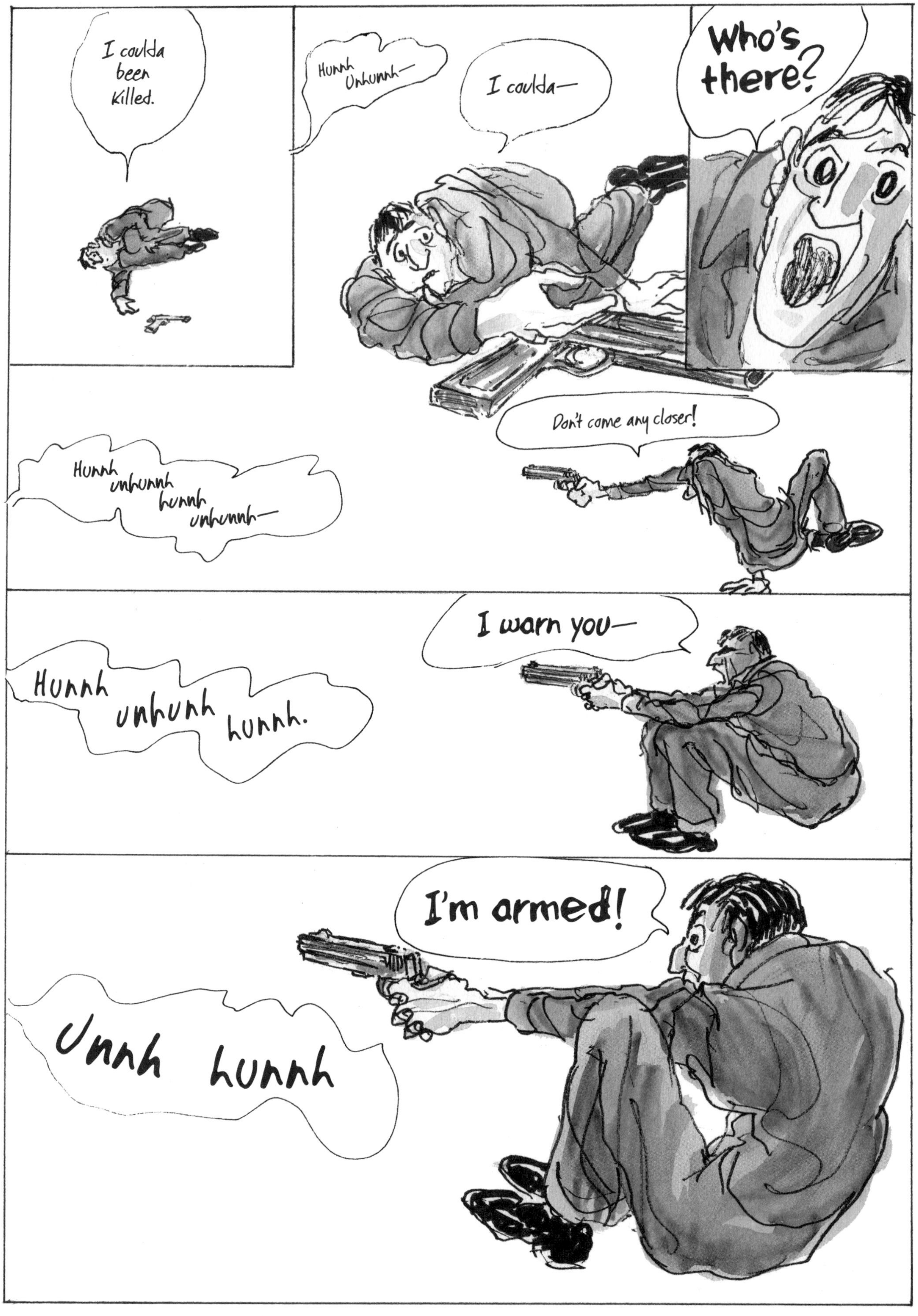
I coulda been killed.
Hunnh Unhunnh—
I coulda—
Who's there?
Don't come any closer!
Hunnh unhunnh hunnh unhunnh—
I warn you—
Hunnh unhunh hunnh.
I'm armed!
Unnh hunnh

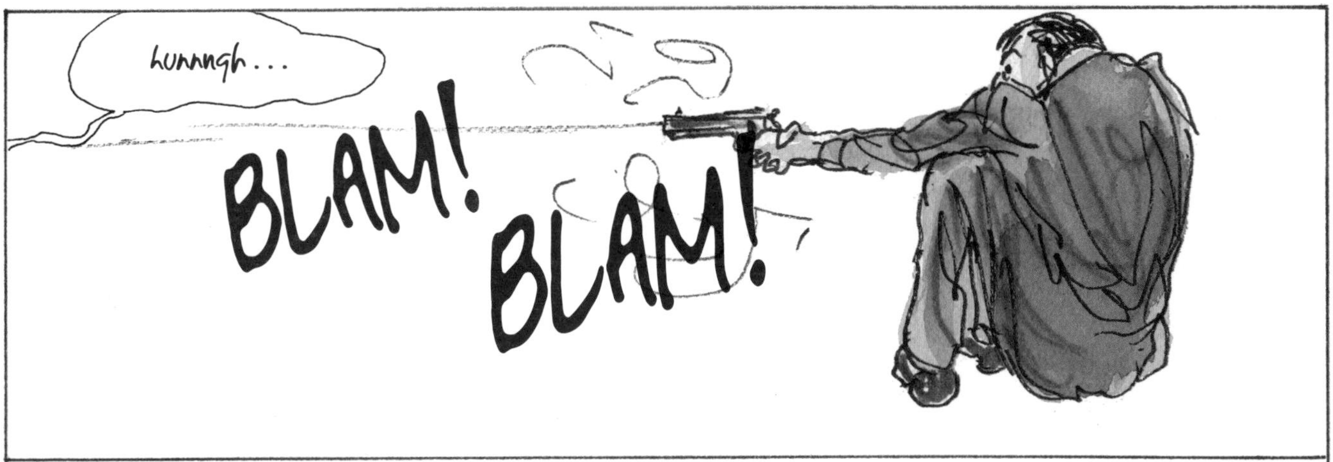
hunnngh...
BLAM! BLAM!

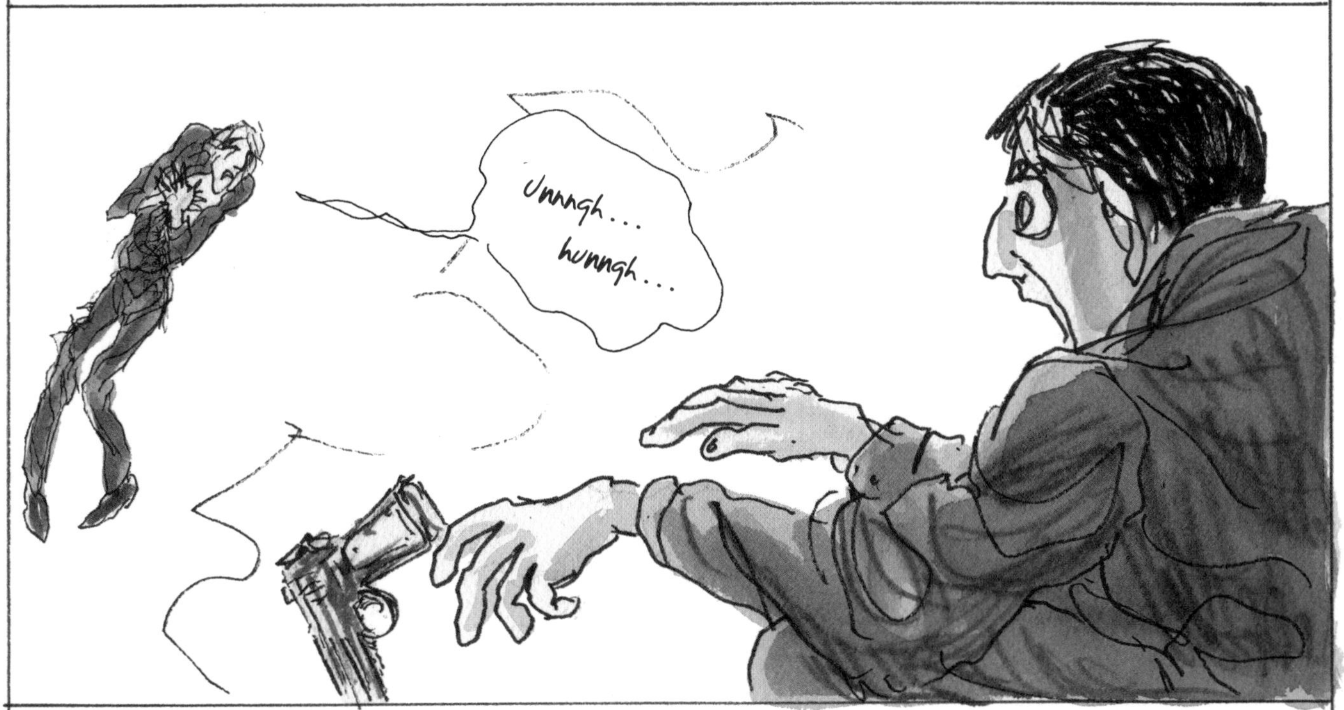
Unnngh... hunngh...

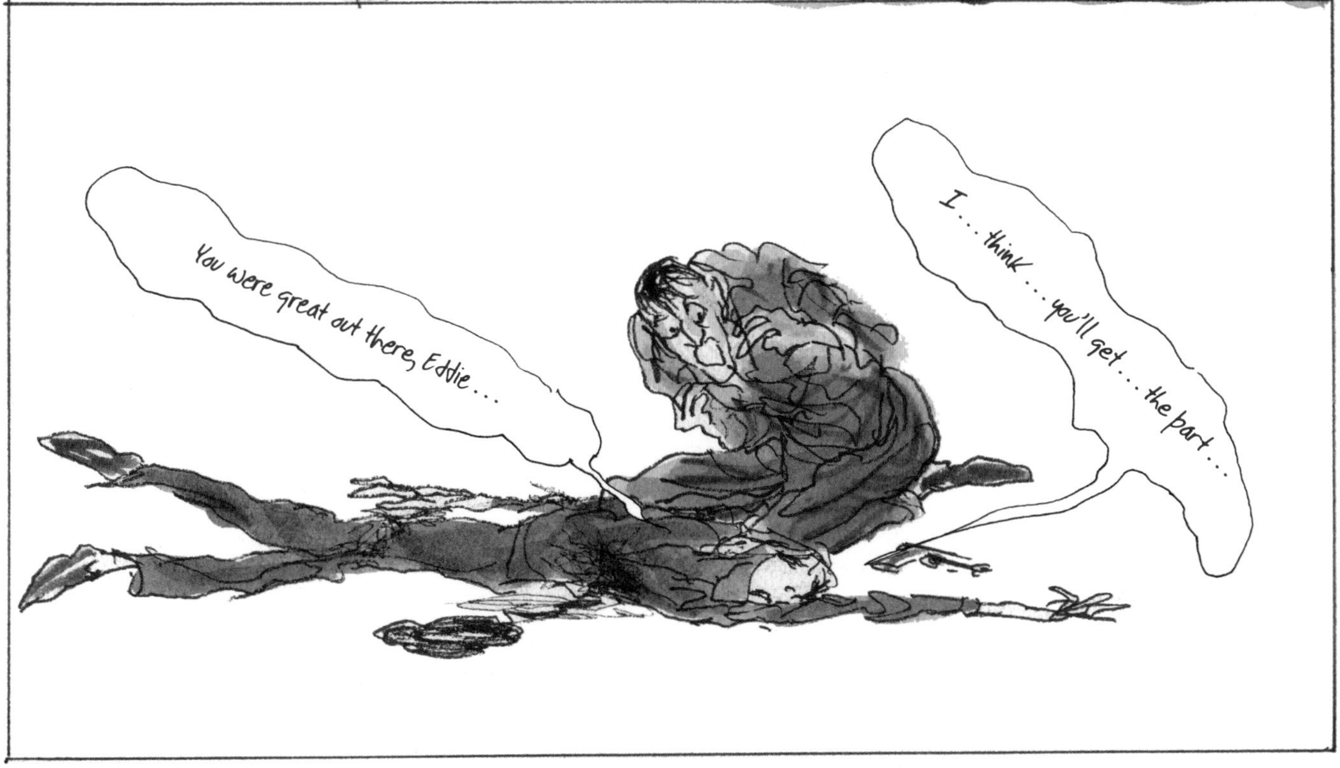
You were great out there, Eddie...
I... think... you'll get... the part...

Chapter Twenty-Three: Visit

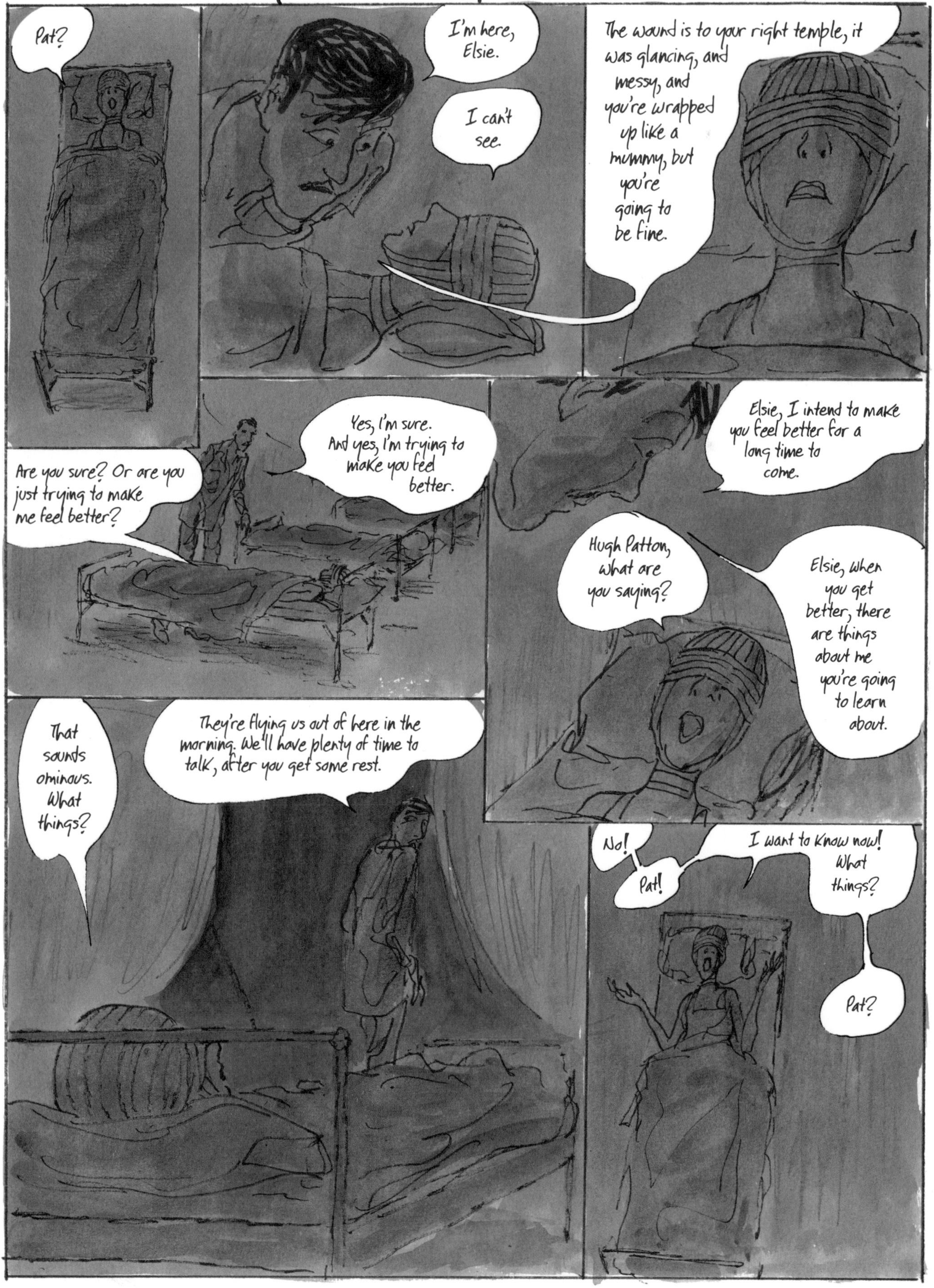
Pat?
I'm here, Elsie.
I can't see.
The wound is to your right temple, it was glancing, and messy, and you're wrapped up like a mummy, but you're going to be fine.
Are you sure? Or are you just trying to make me feel better?
Yes, I'm sure. And yes, I'm trying to make you feel better.
Elsie, I intend to make you feel better for a long time to come.
Hugh Patton, what are you saying?
Elsie, when you get better, there are things about me you're going to learn about.
That sounds ominous. What things?
They're flying us out of here in the morning. We'll have plenty of time to talk, after you get some rest.
No!
Pat!
I want to know now! What things?
Pat?

Chapter Twenty-Four: Revelation

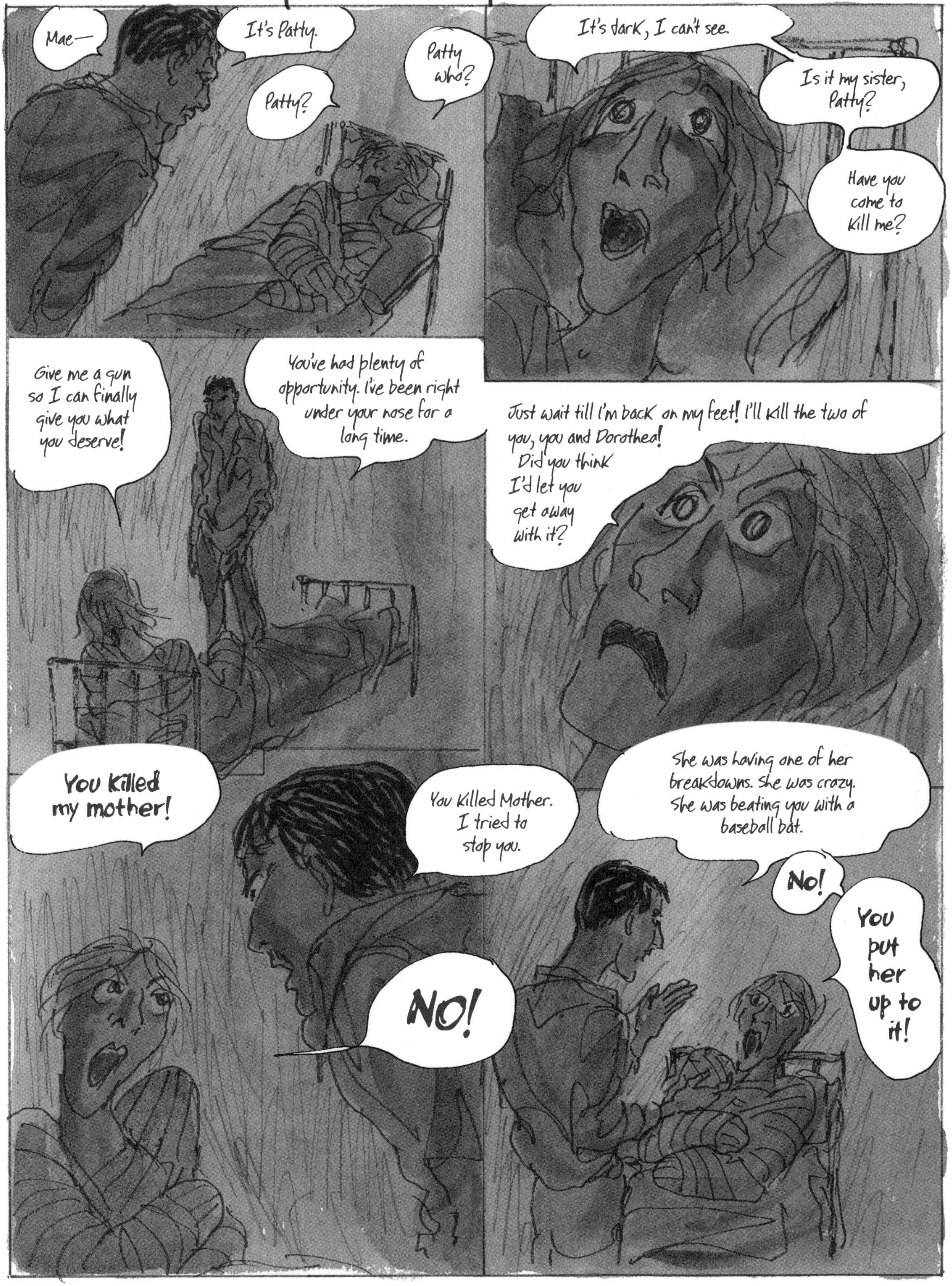

Mae—
It's Patty.
Patty?
Patty who?
It's dark, I can't see.
Is it my sister, Patty?
Have you come to kill me?
Give me a gun so I can finally give you what you deserve!
You've had plenty of opportunity. I've been right under your nose for a long time.
Just wait till I'm back on my feet! I'll kill the two of you, you and Dorothea!
Did you think I'd let you get away with it?
You killed my mother!
You killed Mother. I tried to stop you.
NO!
She was having one of her breakdowns. She was crazy. She was beating you with a baseball bat.
No!
You put her up to it!

136

SCREEN TALK

DANCING DAREDE JOLTS JAP

The flicks' frisky hoofer,
stepped his way into gyrene
front glory Tuesday last whe
for the boys' USO tap-act on the South
atoll, Tarawa, was heckled from the sidelines by
Jap snipers, riddling the star's act with bullets.
But no sneak attack was going to give Eddie the
hook. The dancing whiz onned-with-the-sho
sidestepping hails of bullets to cheers a
retaliation from our boys. Top brag
ward the Fastest Feet Ali
guished Dancing Cross.

Chapter Twenty-Six: Homecoming

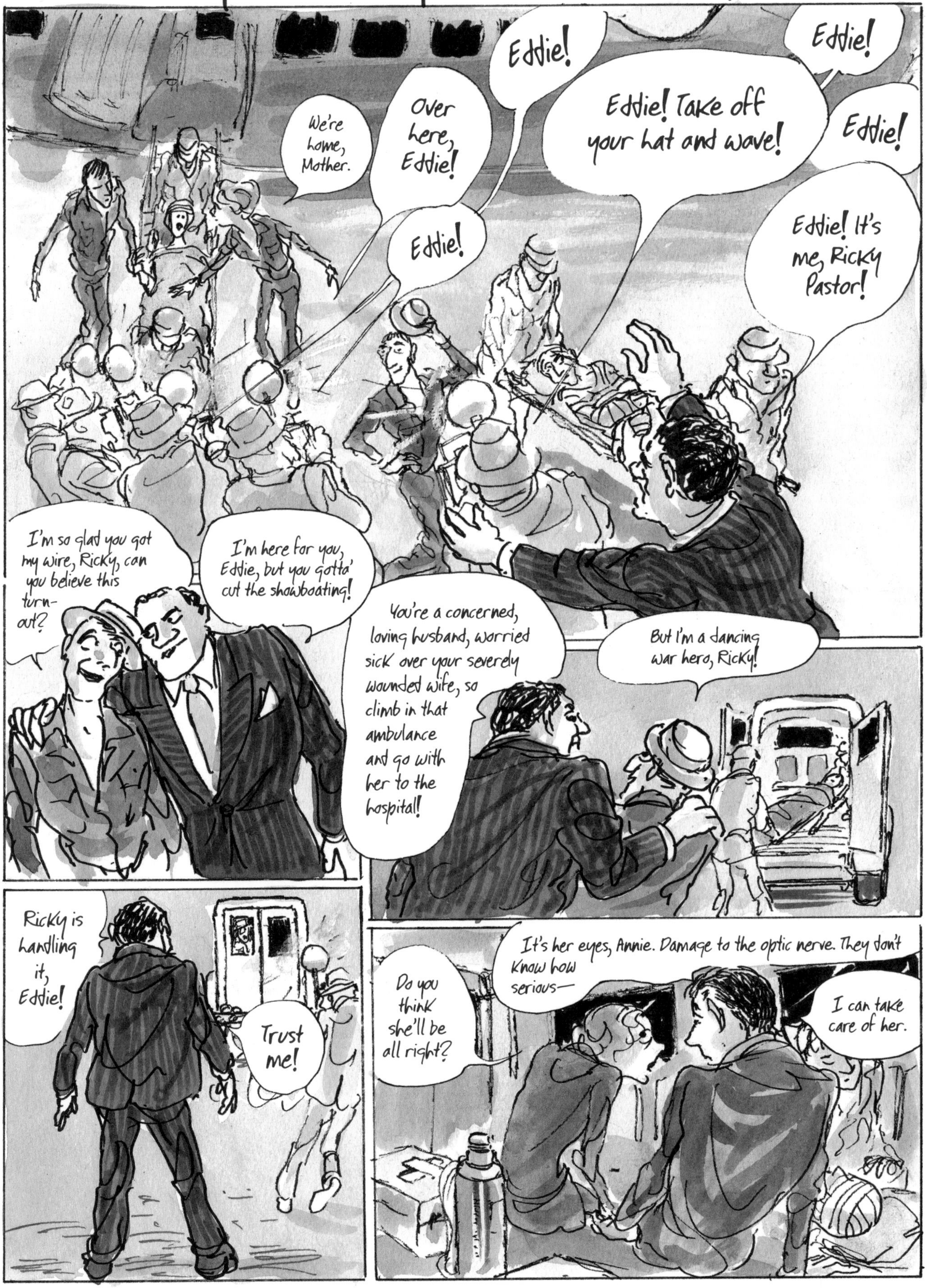
We're home, Mother.
Over here, Eddie!
Eddie!
Eddie!
Eddie! Take off your hat and wave!
Eddie!
Eddie!
Eddie! It's me, Ricky Pastor!
I'm so glad you got my wire, Ricky, can you believe this turn-out?
I'm here for you, Eddie, but you gotta' cut the showboating!
You're a concerned, loving husband, worried sick over your severely wounded wife, so climb in that ambulance and go with her to the hospital!
But I'm a dancing war hero, Ricky!
Ricky is handling it, Eddie!
Trust me!
Do you think she'll be all right?
It's her eyes, Annie. Damage to the optic nerve. They don't know how serious—
I can take care of her.

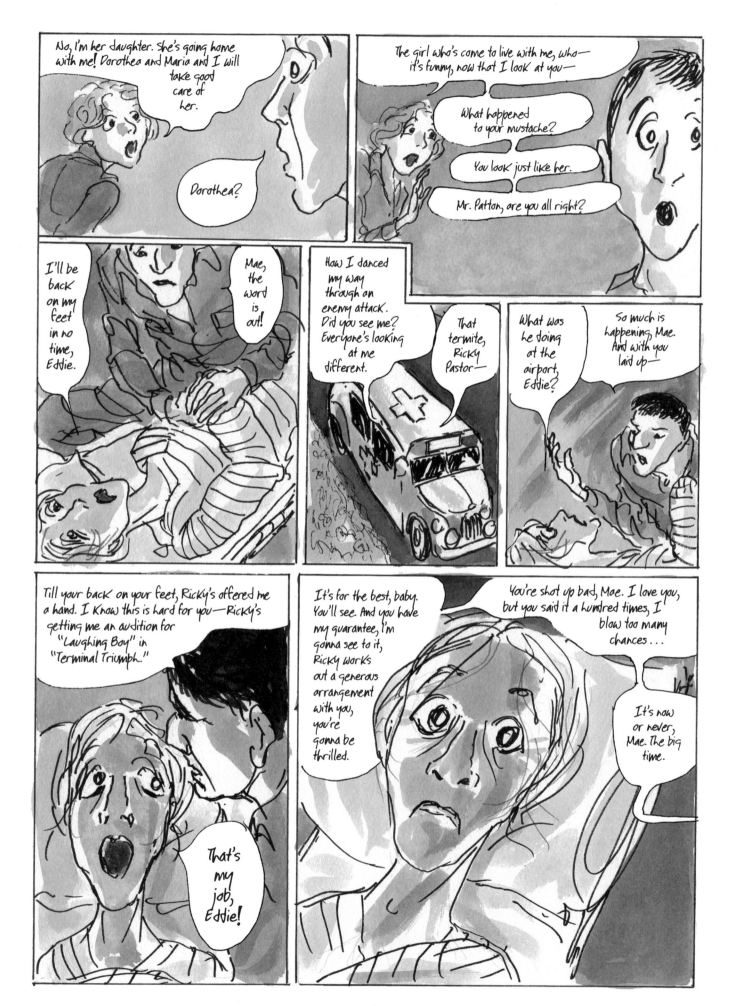

Chapter Twenty-Seven: Kill My Mother

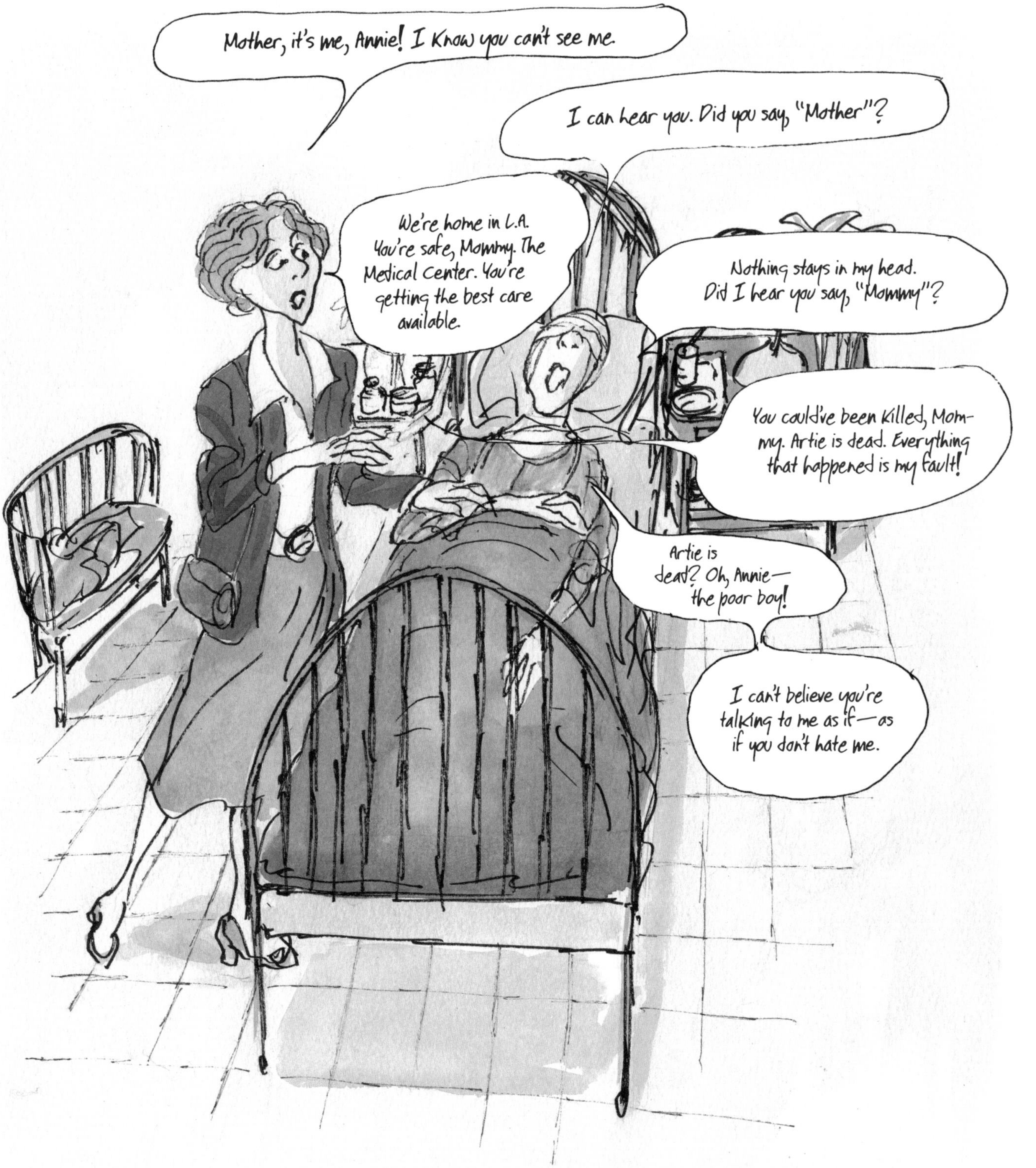
Mother, it's me, Annie! I Know you can't see me.
I can hear you. Did you say, "Mother"?
We're home in L.A. You're safe, Mommy. The Medical Center. You're getting the best care available.
Nothing stays in my head. Did I hear you say, "Mommy"?
You could've been Killed, Mommy. Artie is dead. Everything that happened is my fault!
Artie is dead? Oh, Annie—the poor boy!
I can't believe you're talking to me as if—as if you don't hate me.

Chapter Twenty-Eight: Hugh into Patty

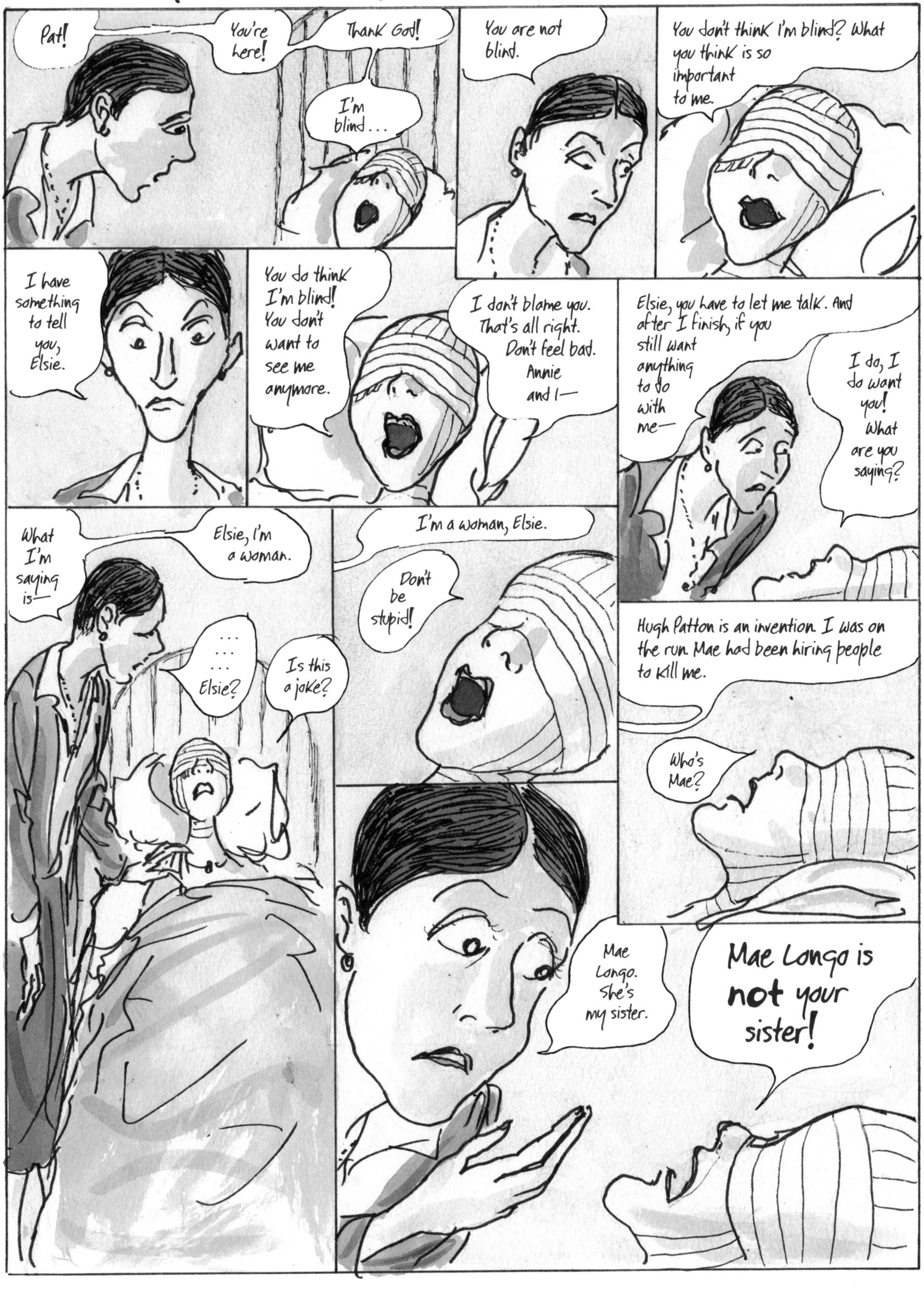

Pat!
You're here!
Thank God!
I'm blind...
You are not blind.
You don't think I'm blind? What you think is so important to me.
I have something to tell you, Elsie.
You do think I'm blind! You don't want to see me anymore.
I don't blame you. That's all right. Don't feel bad. Annie and I—
Elsie, you have to let me talk. And after I finish, if you still want anything to do with me—
I do, I do want you! What are you saying?
What I'm saying is—
Elsie, I'm a woman.
... ... Elsie?
Is this a joke?
I'm a woman, Elsie.
Don't be stupid!
Hugh Patton is an invention. I was on the run. Mae had been hiring people to kill me.
Who's Mae?
Mae Longo. She's my sister.
Mae Longo is **not** your sister!

Chapter Twenty-Nine: Terminal Triumph

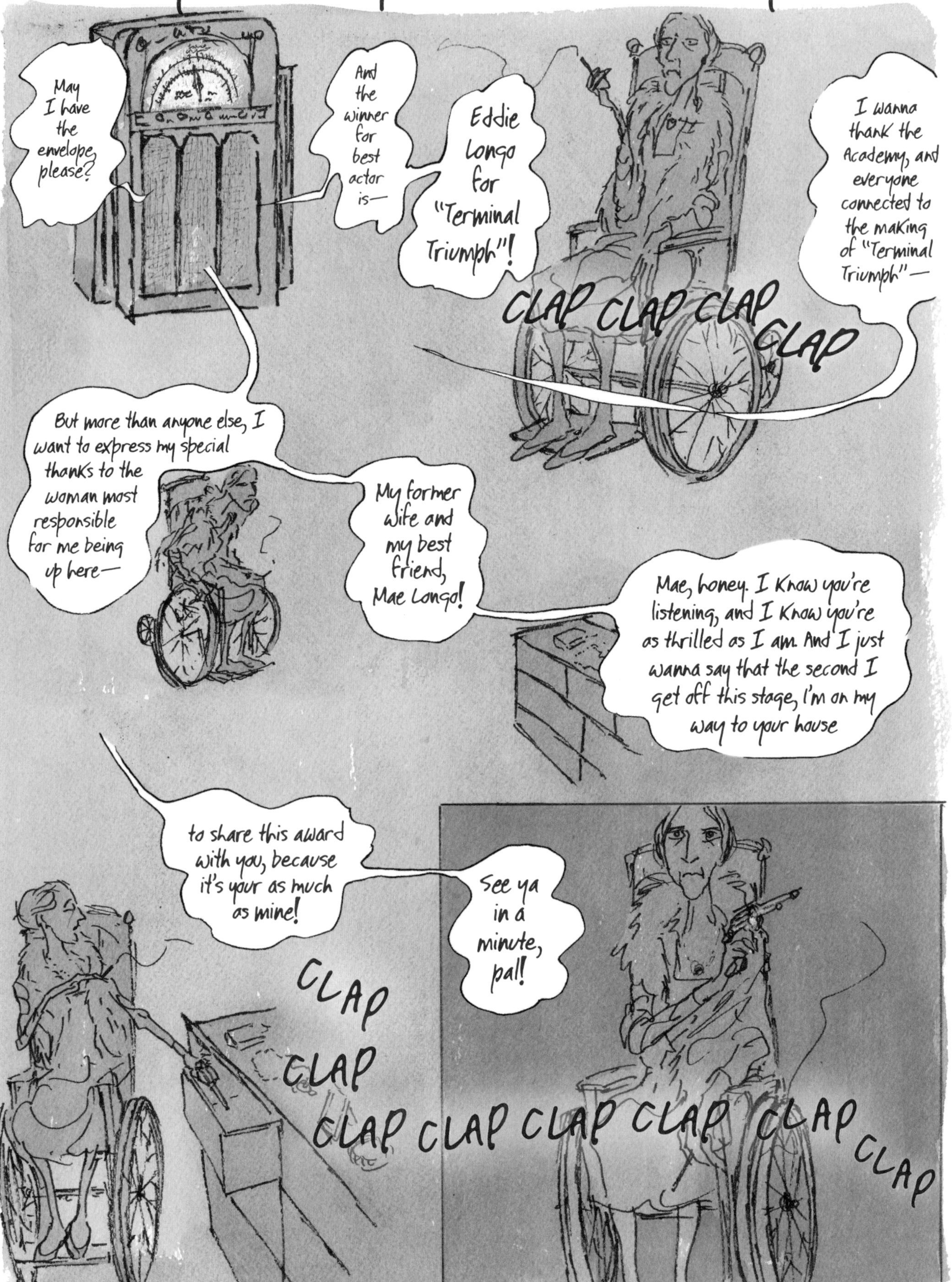

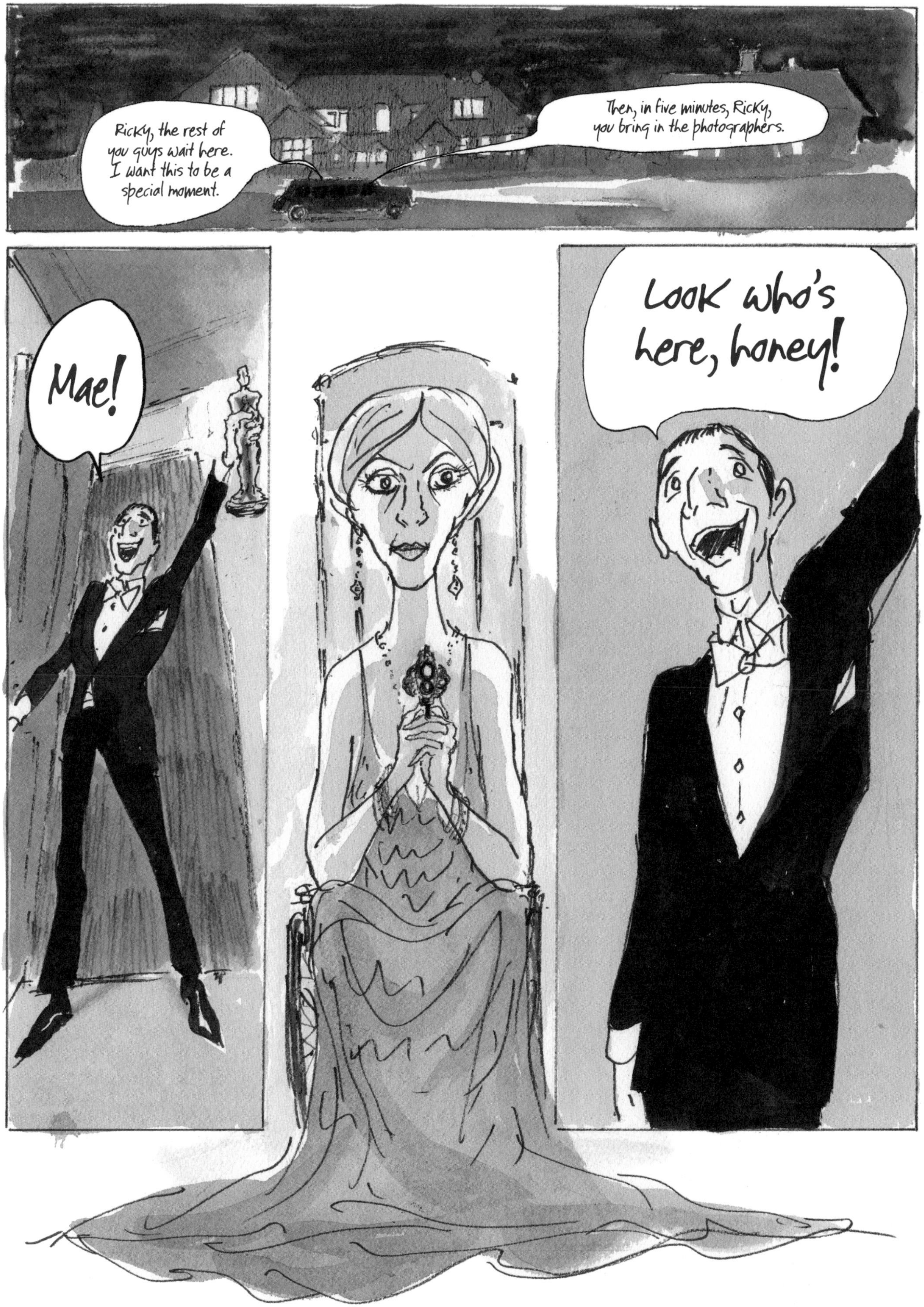
Ricky, the rest of you guys wait here. I want this to be a special moment.
Then, in five minutes, Ricky, you bring in the photographers.
Mae!
Look who's here, honey!

Chapter Thirty: Wrap Party

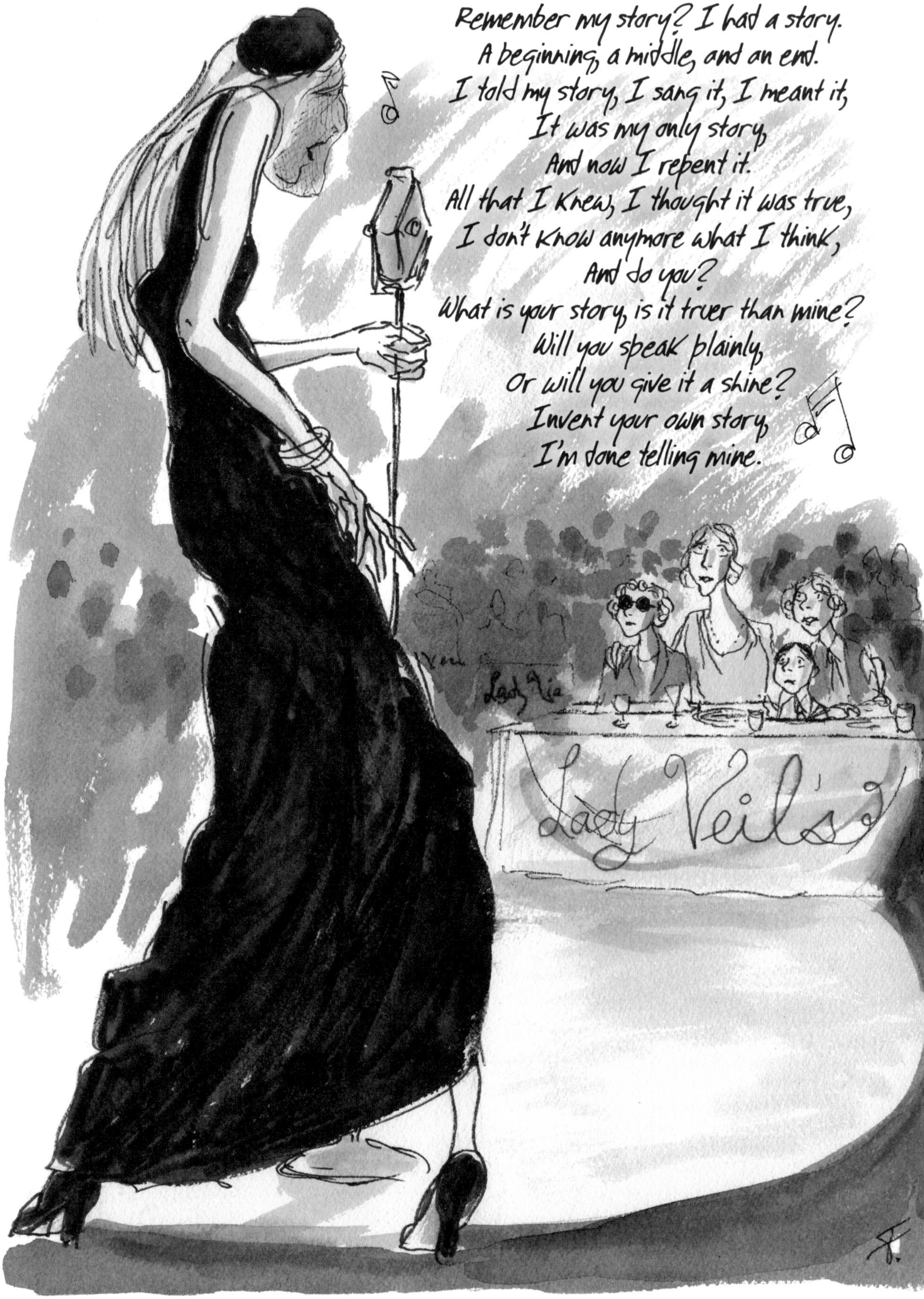
Remember my story? I had a story.
A beginning, a middle, and an end.
I told my story, I sang it, I meant it,
It was my only story,
And now I repent it.
All that I knew, I thought it was true,
I don't know anymore what I think,
And do you?
What is your story, is it truer than mine?
Will you speak plainly,
Or will you give it a shine?
Invent your own story,
I'm done telling mine.
Lady Veil's

Acknowledgments

Victor Giannini typed the first draft and googled photos of thirties cars, street scenes, interiors, and what all.

Tula Holmes typed revisions, ruled and erased pages, googled thirties and forties fashions, World War II uniforms, cars, planes, more what all.

Zelie Rellim typed the final draft, erased pages, googled jungle scenes, forties armaments, hospital interiors, Hollywood exteriors and interiors, even more what all.

Turner Classic Movies, plus a 65-inch Blu-ray high-definition flat screen, and the pause button on my remote, so that I could re-create the look of noir. No problem. It posed for me.

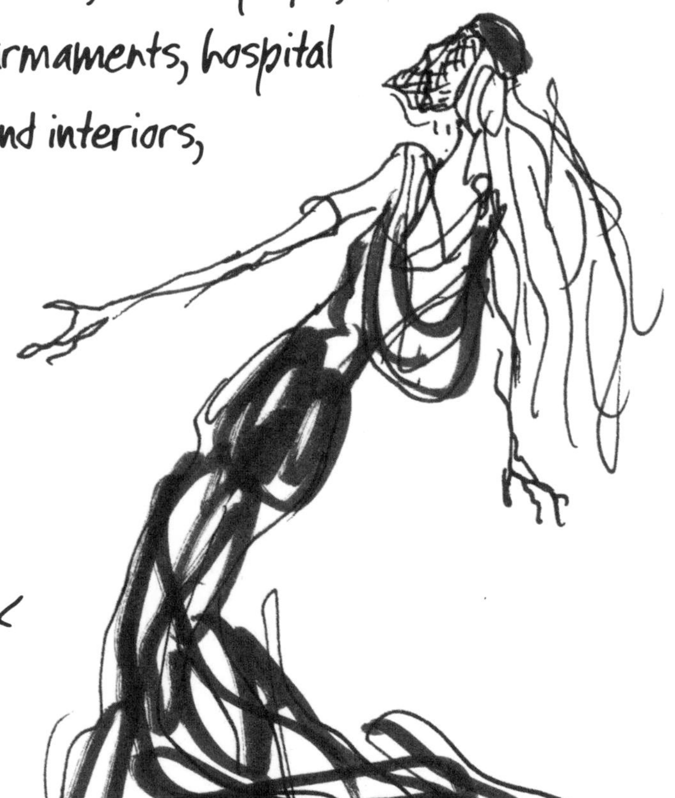